Celestial
Charts

For David, Ellen and Owen
With love

Celestial Charts

Antique Maps of the Heavens

by
CAROLE STOTT

STUDIO EDITIONS

LONDON

Acknowledgements

The author wishes to express her thanks to the staff of the museums and libraries who care for the celestial charts depicted in this book. Everyone was very helpful in assisting her work. Special thanks to Robert Baldwin, Brian Thynne, Richard Dummett, Kristen Lippincott and the photographic staff, David Spence, Jim Stevenson, Barrie Cash, Keith Percival and Tina Chambers, at the National Maritime Museum, London; to David Hughes at Sheffield University; and to Peter Hingley and Mary Chibnall at the Royal Astronomical Society, London. The largest thank-you goes to Robert Baldwin who, as always, was especially generous in sharing his time and knowledge.

First published 1991 by Studio Editions Ltd.
Princess House, 50 Eastcastle Street
London W1N 7AP, England.

Copyright this edition © Studio Editions Ltd., 1991

The right of Carole Stott to be identified as author of this work has been asserted by her in accordance with the Copyright, Designs and Patents Act, 1988.

ISBN 1-8517-0626-7

Printed and bound in Hong Kong

Contents

Prospectus Tertius Globi Cœlestis ab Atlante Farnesiano suffulti, respondens posteri statuæ, oculo constituto in plano Coluri Aequinoctiorum, et inspectante sectionem Autumnalem. ABC. Circulus Ascensionis rectæ ductus per luci lam in Cornu Arietis et per genua Asterismi Virginis D sectio Autumnalis DB Præcessio Aequinoctiorum ætate Ptolemæi EF Circulus Aequinoctialis GH Tropicus Aestivus IK Tropicus Hyemalis LMN Circulus nusquam apparentium Maximus in lati tudine graduum 40 Asterismi. 1 Bootes 2 Corona Boreæ 3 Hercules 4 Serpentarius 5 Leo 6 Virgo 7 Libra 8 Chelæ Scorpionis. 9 Scorpii cauda 10 Hydri pars 11 Vas 12 Corvus 13 Centaurus 14 Lupus 15 Ara 16 Corona Australis 17 Navis.

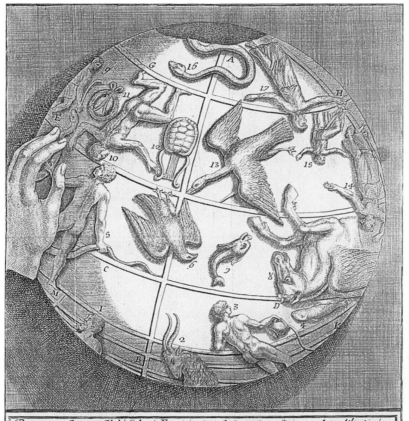

Prospectus Quartus Globi Cœlestis Farnesiani, oculo inspectante Sinistrum latus Atlantis a quo fulcitur AB Colurus Solstitiorum CD Circulus Aequinoctialis EF Tropicus Cancri GN Circulus Sem per apparentium maximus in latitudine grad 40 M BK Ecliptica Asterismi 1 Sagittarii pars 2 Capricorni pars 3 Aquarius 4 Piscis Boreus 5 Serpentarius 6 Aquila 7 Delphinus 8 Pegasus 9 Bootes 10 Hercules 11 Corona Borealis 12 Lyra 13 Cygnus 14 Andromeda 15 Cassiopea 16 Draco 17 Cepheus.

The *Farnese Atlas*, 200 BC, from the National Maritime Museum, London. The Museo Nazionale in Naples houses a marble statue of the mythological character, Atlas, who supports the heavens on his shoulders. These two broadsheets from the *Farnese Atlas* show the celestial globe with some of its constellations: the hands on either side represent the hands of Atlas.

INTRODUCTION

oday we know and understand much more about our world than did ancient man. Yet even today the night sky retains for us its mystery and fascination, whether we respond simply to the natural romance of the stars or to the intellectual challenge they present.

Let man master the sky and what it contains, and he shall hold the key to the Universe itself. Ancient man took his first steps in understanding the heavens when he designed a system for recognising the stars. He grouped the stars together, using the patterns they formed as a home for the figures of myth, as a means of finding his way about the sky, and as a backdrop for the movements of other astronomical bodies. At a stroke man had transformed the sky from a confusion of twinkling lights into an ordered system of stars.

Through the course of the centuries some of the star patterns or constellations became generally accepted. As astronomical observation improved, and, as more stars were measured and catalogued, the list of constellations was refined and extended. Astronomers today use an internationally accepted set of constellations. The celestial charts in this book illustrate the story behind the choice of our present constellations. In the main the illustrations reproduced here are of printed star maps, produced after 1515, the date of the very first printed star map. The earlier manuscript drawings of the constellations set the scene. Later on in the book, single sheet maps, atlases and globes reveal the development of the more recent, additional constellations. By the nineteenth century, the days of the beautiful celestial charts were numbered. Professional astronomers no longer required constellation pictures on their maps; they preferred a less cluttered, more scientific image, presenting stellar position and identity with accuracy and clarity. In the nineteenth century the more attractive maps and the increasing number of movable planispheres were produced for the grow-

ing market of amateur stargazers. By the early years of the twentieth century, celestial maps of both types had become increasingly utilitarian, and the set of present day constellations had become established.

It is impossible to pinpoint exactly when the first constellations were devised. Ancient man learnt very quickly that the motion of the Sun across the sky affected his life. It produced his day, formed the seasons, and measured out his year. In order to understand and follow the course of the Sun's path, he mapped the stars which form the backdrop to the Sun's movement. The band of sky centred on the Sun's path became known as the zodiac. The stars within this band were divided into twelve constellation groupings: the zodiac constellations. The Sun completes one circuit of its path – the ecliptic – in one year, passing through a specific zodiac constellation each month. In ancient times, for example, the Sun crossed the constellation of Aries between March 21 and April 21. The Moon and the planets also move within the zodiac band of sky. Consequently the twelve zodiac signs – Aries, Taurus, Gemini, Cancer, Leo, Virgo, Libra, Scorpius, Sagittarius, Capricornus, Aquarius and Pisces – were amongst the first constellations to be devised. With the exception of Libra, the scales, which was a later addition, the zodiac signs are all living creatures. The term 'zodiac' derives from the Greek word for 'animal'.

The stars that make up the zodiac constellations can be seen, through the course of a year, from any point on Earth. Other constellations further to the north or the south of the zodiac band are, in general, only observed as the stargazer moves his position increasingly to the north or south of the Earth's equator. The portion of sky available for observation is directly related to the observer's latitude. What the observer actually sees within that space depends on the time of year and the time of night. A constellation system for the more northerly stars, devised by Mediterranean and Arabic peoples, was the first to be developed. It was not until European explorers travelled further south that the southern stars were catalogued and formed into constellations. The development of the southern constellations is well-documented. The history of the northern, older, constellations is more difficult to trace. We cannot say for certain when individual constellations were formed, but there is evidence which shows how early in our history a framework of constellations was established.

Around 150 AD, the Alexandrian astronomer, Claudius Ptolemaeus (Ptolemy as he is more usually known) produced the *Almagest*. This was destined to become one of the most significant books in the history of astronomy. A handbook of mathematical astronomy, it collated the astronomical knowledge of the ancient world. The *Almagest* contains a star catalogue listing a total of 1,028 stars (1,025 plus three duplicates). All these stars could be seen with the naked eye from the Mediterranean countries. Ptolemy divided these stars into forty-eight constellations. We have already met the twelve zodiac constellations. There were also twenty-one constellations to the north of the zodiac, and fifteen to the south. The constellations were not devised by Ptolemy; he was simply basing his work on ancient tradition and earlier star catalogues, such as that produced by Hipparchus, a Greek astronomer of the second century BC. The earlier works no longer exist, but study has shown that we can trace forty-three of the constella-

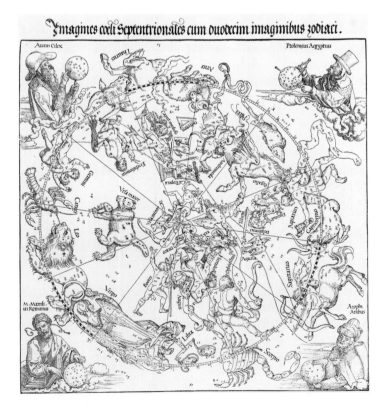

The northern celestial sky by Albrecht Dürer, 1515. This, together with its southern sky companion, were the first printed star charts.

brightest star in a constellation is usually termed α, the second brightest β (beta) and so on through the Greek alphabet. The letter is commonly known as the Bayer letter because the system was introduced by Johann Bayer in his star atlas *Uranometria* published in 1603. This system has, however, its faults. In some constellations the brightest star is not the one designated α; in the constellation Orion, for example, the brightest star is in fact termed β.

The Italian astronomer, Alessandro Piccolomini, introduced a similar system some years earlier in his star atlas of 1540 where the significant stars were identified by letters from the Latin alphabet. The brightest was usually designated 'A'. However, it was Bayer's system that was copied by other mapmakers and adopted by astronomers. John Flamsteed gave his name to another star identification system. Flamsteed numbers identify a star according to its right ascension within a constellation. The greater the right ascension of the star, the higher the number used to identify it. Today the system is used to mark faint naked-eye stars.

Where stars have individual names, these may appear on the maps. In popular culture the names would be better known than Bayer letters. Generally, a name pre-dates any other system of star identification. The example already noted, α Canis Majoris, is well known as Sirius, a name of Greek origin, used by Ptolemy. Other names passed on to us by Ptolemy include Arcturus (α Boötes), Capella (α Aurigae), Antares (α Scorpio) and Canopus (α Carinae) some of the brightest stars in the sky.

Ptolemy's other means of identifying a star was to outline its position within a constellation. For example, the star now known as Fomalhaut was described by Ptolemy as 'the one in the mouth', the mouth, that is, of Piscis Austrini, the constellation of the southern fish. The *Almagest* was translated into Arabic in the eighth and ninth centuries, the descriptions being slightly affected by the translation. Similarly, the westernised versions of Arabic names in use today can bear little resemblance to the original Arabic meaning. Some names are more truly Arabic, whilst others reflect an Arabic origin. Variants of star names appear on the maps. Even today, with more than two hundred Arabic star names in common use, inconsistencies abound.

Many of the maps and charts in this book include a stellar brightness scale in which the size of the star symbol relates to the brightness of the star. A star appears bright to us on Earth either because it is close or because it is giving out lots of energy. The brightness of a star is expressed in terms of its magnitude (i.e. importance). The brightest stars in the sky are of the first magnitude and the faintest stars visible to the naked eye are of the sixth magnitude. The magnitude of a star indicates to the stargazer just how easily a star can be seen by an observer on Earth.

Hipparchus, working in the second century BC, classified the stars he observed in terms of brightness. He described the twenty brightest stars as of first importance, the faintest stars of sixth importance. The intermediate stars were given values of 2, 3, 4 and 5, depending on their brightness. Hipparchus' values have now been converted into a numerical scale of apparent magnitudes. Again the larger the number, the fainter the star. From the 1850s the brightness ratio between a star of first magnitude and one of sixth magnitude has been fixed at exactly one hundred. This means that for each integer step along the apparent magnitude scale a star is either 2.512 brighter or fainter than the classification next to it.

The constellation of Cygnus, from *De Le Stelle Fisse Libro Uno* by Alessandro Piccolomini, published in 1540. Piccolomini's book is the first printed collection of star maps (as distinct from constellation drawings), and can thus be regarded as the first printed star atlas.

Stars other than single stars can be highlighted within a constellation. To the early astronomer, as to the novice observer today, the sky seems to be just studded with pinpoints of light which are apparently single, unchanging stars. We now know differently. Some stars are actually made up of two stars placed very close together. Of these, many may be true double stars; a double star is a partnership in the sky where both stars orbit their common centre of gravity. Other stars are variable, their brightness varying over a period of time as the star pulsates. New classifications of stars and star groupings, such as clusters and galaxies, were included on the star charts, as they were identified.

European astronomers used sighting tubes to improve the accuracy with which they measured coordinates. Even before the telescope was first turned on the heavens by Galileo Galilei in 1609, other astronomers and navigators had explored the southern skies by voyaging south, listing and then charting the stars. The Dutch navigators, Pietr Dirksz Keyser and Frederick de Houtman, were the first of the Europeans to chart the stars centred on the southern celestial pole. Their work was later supplemented by that of the Englishman, Edmond Halley, and, more permanently, by the work of a Frenchman, Nicolas Louis de Lacaille. At the turn of the sixteenth century, the work of the Dutch navigators led to the introduction of twelve new constellations which are still in use today. These were largely based on the exotic animals discovered on the voyages of exploration, for example, the bird of paradise, the chamaelon and tucan. Another fourteen constellations were added by Lacaille in 1754. With the exception of Mensa, named after the Table Mountain where he carried out his observations, all fourteen feature some tool or instrument used in the arts or sciences; for example, the clock, microscope, painter's easel and engraving tool. All can still be found in the sky today. A few new, northern hemisphere constellations were even introduced, such as those of Hevelius who grouped together some of the fainter stars between the existing constellations. These have also come into regular use.

Many completely new constellation designations were proposed. These were often ingenious and striking, but were not popularly acclaimed and so reigned only briefly. Proposals ranged from single constellations, to entirely new schemes that would totally redesign the heavens. The most notable revision was that of Julius Schiller who turned the twelve zodiac constellations into the twelve apostles, while the northern and southern constellations were represented by figures from the New and Old Testaments.

The eighty-eight constellations in use today were officially and internationally adopted by the astronomical community at the first General Assembly of the International Astronomical Union (IAU), held in 1922. Boundaries between the constellations were also settled. Up until this time, as shown by the examples in this book, individual mapmakers drew their own wavy lines between the constellations. However, in 1930, the star maps reproduced in *Delimitation Scientifique des Constellations* displayed the new boundaries drawn along lines of equal right ascension and declination.

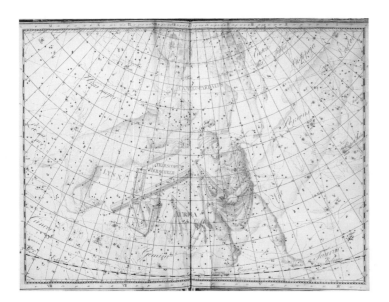

Johannes Bode's atlas of 1801 was the last of the great celestial atlases to combine the skills of both artist and scientist.

Table of Constellations

Name	Common Name	Name	Common Name	Name	Common Name
Andromeda*	Andromeda	Crux	The Southern Cross	Orion*	Orion, the Hunter
Antlia	The Air Pump	Cygnus*	The Swan	Pavo	The Peacock
Apus	The Bird of Paradise	Delphinus*	The Dolphin	Pegasus*	Pegasus
Aquarius*	The Water Carrier	Dorado	The Goldfish	Perseus*	Perseus
Aquila*	The Eagle	Draco*	The Dragon	Phoenix	The Phoenix
Ara*	The Altar	Equuleus*	The Little Horse	Pictor	The Painter's Easel
Aries*	The Ram	Eridanus*	The River Eridanus	Pisces*	The Fishes
Auriga*	The Charioteer	Fornax	The Furnace	Piscis Austrinus*	The Southern Fish
Boötes*	The Herdsman	Gemini*	The Twins	Puppis	The Stern
Caelum	The Engraving Tool	Grus	The Crane	Pyxis	The Mariner's Compass
Camelopardalis	The Giraffe	Hercules*	Hercules	Reticulum	The Net
Cancer*	The Crab	Horologium	The Pendulum Clock	Sagitta*	The Arrow
Canes Venatici	The Hunting Dogs	Hydra*	The Water Snake	Sagittarius*	The Archer
Canis Major*	The Greater Dog	Hydrus	The Lesser Water Snake	Scorpius*	The Scorpion
Canis Minor*	The Lesser Dog	Indus	The Indian	Sculptor	The Sculptor
Capricornus*	The Sea Goat	Lacerta	The Lizard	Scutum	The Shield
Carina	The Keel	Leo*	The Lion	Serpens*	The Serpent
Cassiopeia*	Cassiopeia	Leo Minor	The Lesser Lion	Sextans	The Sextant
Centaurus*	The Centaur	Lepus*	The Hare	Taurus*	The Bull
Cepheus*	Cepheus	Libra*	The Scales	Telescopium	The Telescope
Cetus*	The Whale	Lupus*	The Wolf	Triangulum*	The Triangle
Chamaeleon	The Chameleon	Lynx	The Lynx	Triangulum Australe	The Southern Triangle
Circinus	The Pair of Compasses	Lyra*	The Lyre	Tucana	The Toucan
Columba	The Dove	Mensa	Table Mountain	Ursa Major*	The Great Bear
Coma Berenices	Berenice's Hair	Microscopium	The Microscope	Ursa Minor*	The Lesser Bear
Corona Australis*	The Southern Crown	Monoceros	The Unicorn	Vela	The Sail
Corona Borealis*	The Northern Crown	Musca	The Fly	Virgo*	The Virgin
Corvus*	The Crow	Norma	The Level	Volans	The Flying Fish
Crater*	The Cup	Octans	The Octant	Vulpecula	The Fox
		Ophiuchus*	The Serpent Holder		

* Forty-seven Ptolemaic constellations. The forty-eighth Argo Navis,
is now represented by Carina, Puppis and Vela.

The Ptolemaic view of the universe

from Atlas Coelestis seu Harmonica Macrocosmica *by Andreas Cellarius, Amsterdam, 1661. Plate size 20.75 × 17.5 in.*

The universe is everything there is: the Earth, our star the Sun and its nine planets, all the other stars, the Milky Way galaxy, and all other galaxies. Our present knowledge of what the universe consists of and how its parts are arranged stems mainly from the work of twentieth-century astronomers. At the time of the publication of the first star charts, in the early sixteenth century, man's picture of the universe was quite different. The universe was then believed to consist of the Earth, the Sun and Moon, five other planets – Mercury, Venus, Mars, Jupiter and Saturn – and the stars beyond. The Earth was at the centre of the universe,

with everything orbiting about it. This view is represented in this illustration published by Andreas Cellarius at a time when this belief was becoming obsolete.

The Earth and the elements of water, air and fire appear in the centre. Moving outwards we come to the Moon in its orbit, followed by Mercury, Venus, the Sun, Mars, Jupiter and Saturn revolving in their orbits. They are all named and represented by their symbols. Small tableaux show something of the character of the individual planets. Mars – the armour-clad Roman god of war – is driving his blood-red chariot, and the beautiful Venus – goddess of love – reclines on her swan-drawn throne of gold. At the very edge of the universe is the sphere of the stars, here represented by the twelve zodiacal constellations accompanied by their names and signs.

The Ptolemaic view of the universe

from Atlas Coelestis seu Harmonica Macrocosmica *by Andreas Cellarius, Amsterdam, 1661. Plate size 20.75 × 17.5 in.*

The Earth-centred (geocentric) theory of the universe is known as the Ptolemaic system, after the Alexandria-based astronomer Claudius Ptolemaeus, known as Ptolemy, who described it in the second century BC. His *Almagest*, a great compendium of contemporary astronomical knowledge, consisting of both Greek astronomy to his own day and his own original work, is one of the most significant books in the history of astronomy. As well as this long-lasting theory of the universe, it provided the basis for our present system of constellations. Its star catalogue listed 1,025 stars

visible to observers in the lands around the Mediterranean sea. These were formed into 48 constellations, which, with little modification, are still in use today.

The Ptolemaic understanding of the universe satisfied the astronomical world until the sixteenth century. Alternative views then began to be put forward, and by the seventeenth century a sun-centred (heliocentric) system took precedence. This in turn became the basis of the view of the universe held by astronomers today.

This illustration of the Ptolemaic system reflects the dominant, central role that was ascribed to the Earth. The known planets, the Moon and the Sun orbit around it. The sphere of the stars, represented here by the constellations of the zodiac, marks the edge of the Ptolemaic universe.

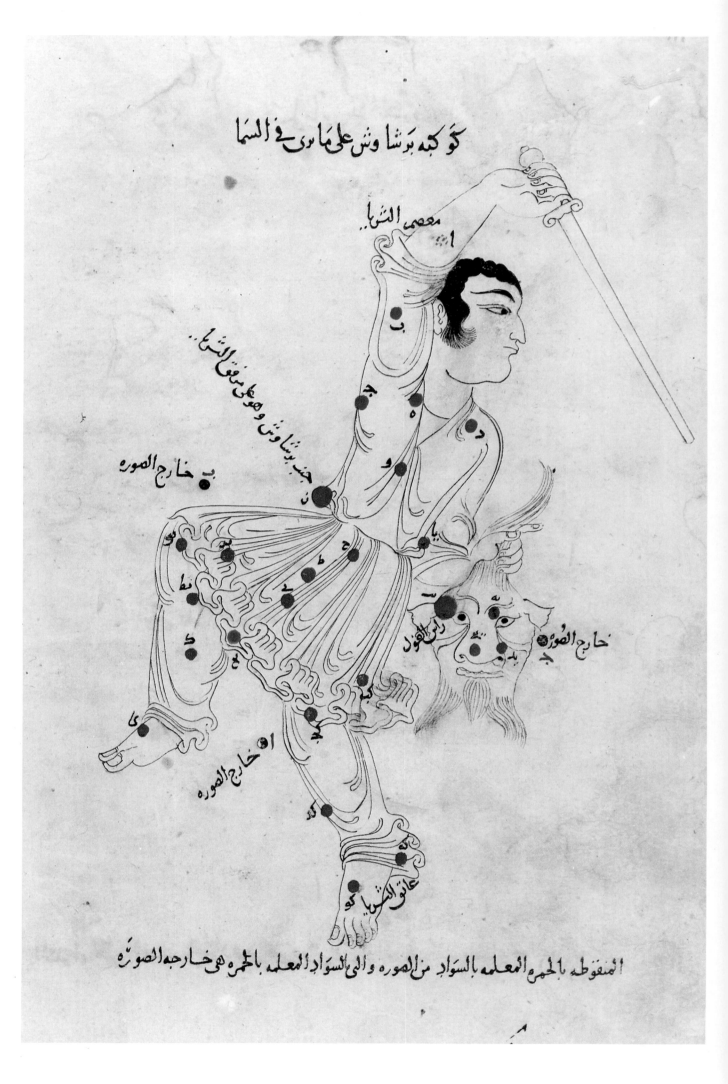

The constellations of Perseus and Andromeda *from the manuscript* Book of Fixed Stars *by Al Sufi. Bodleian Library, Oxford, Manuscript Marsh 144.*

Claudius Ptolemy's great work *Almagest* had been translated into Arabic by the ninth century. The *Book of Fixed Stars* follows the pattern of Ptolemy's book, describing the celestial constellations, and listing the stars. This 419 page work is ascribed to the Arab astronomer, Abd al-Rahman b.Umar al-Sufi; it was dedicated to his friend and pupil, the Buyid Sultan Adud al-Dawlah, tenth century ruler of Iraq.

Each constellation is illustrated twice: as it appears in the sky, viewed from Earth, and also as it would appear if viewed from outside the celestial sphere, as though on a globe. The black-ink constellations are drawn around the red stars. Other close, but non-constellation stars appear in black. Important stars are identified by name.

The constellations reproduced here show Perseus and Andromeda as they would appear in the sky. They are celestial neighbours and share their story with adjacent constellations. Andromeda, who is chained to a rock as a sacrifice to the sea monster, Cetus, is the daughter of Cepheus and Cassiopeia, the king and queen of Ethiopia. The beautiful and helpless Andromeda attracts the attention of Perseus who has

recently beheaded the gorgon, Medusa. Perseus successfully slays the monster, rescues Andromeda and takes her as his bride.

Al Sufi's figures follow their classical originals with some modifications. These changes could be due both to a misunderstanding of the mythology of the figures and to the oriental influence. Perseus, at left, carries not Medusa's head but that of a bearded male demon. Both figures have oriental faces, clothes and jewellery, and are drawn in a distinctively flat style. This illustration of Andromeda is one of three in Al Sufi's book. It shows her with arms and hands outstretched, symbolising the enchained woman. The two fishes across her chest are additions to the classical figure, reflecting the influence of the stellar system of the Bedouin tribes which was quite separate from that of the Greeks.

The celestial sphere
from Atlas Coelestis seu
Harmonica Macrocosmica *by*
Andreas Cellarius,
Amsterdam, 1661. Plate size
20.75 × 17.5 in.

Astronomers use a
framework of imaginary
lines and circles to divide up
the sky, and the positions of
the stars and other heavenly
bodies are measured with
reference to this framework.
The divisions of the sky and
its principal points are
shown here as they would
appear to an observer living
on Earth at latitude 45
degrees north. The spin axis
of the Earth goes from top
right to bottom left. At the
top right of the diagram, the
north celestial pole can be
seen directly above the
Earth's northern pole. Notice
also that the Earth's north
celestial pole is 45 degrees
above the observer's
horizon.

The extension of the
Earth's equator intersects the
sky as the celestial equator.

TERRÆ COELESTIBVS DATÆ.

The northern and southern tropics of Cancer and Capricorn are also clearly marked, as are the Arctic and Antarctic polar circles. Directly above the observer is his zenith, whereas below his feet, at the bottom of this diagram, appears his nadir. The zodiacal band girdles the sky and is inclined at 23½ degrees to the equator.

The sky map is surrounded by a host of putti, one of whom holds a cross-staff (upper left) while others carry mariner's astrolabes. Mariners used this type of astrolabe to make altitude observations of stars which in turn would enable them to establish their latitude. At lower right is an armillary sphere – a three-dimensional model of the heavens in which brass rings represent the various imaginary lines and circles that make up the celestial sphere. The central globe of the Earth and the broad band that represents the ecliptic are easily seen here.

The constellations of Draco and Aquarius
from De Sideribus Tractatus *by Gaius Julius Hyginus, Italy, c.1450. Page size 9.25 × 6 in.*

The stories of Greek mythology were gathered together by Gaius Julius Hyginus in the second century BC. His *Poeticon Astronomicon* is a collection of the Greek star myths. Hyginus' writings were popular in the Middle Ages, and several illustrated manuscripts reproduced his work. Hyginus' work was published by Erhard Ratdolt in 1482. The printed book included woodcut drawings of the constellations, and proved so popular that it was reissued a number of times.

A mid-fifteenth-century manuscript book following Hyginus' work includes particularly colourful and finely drawn depictions of the Ptolemaic constellations. The constellations of Draco and Aquarius are reproduced here. Draco, the dragon, can

stellas duas obscuras. In utrisq̃ humeris singulas
magnas in sinistro cubitu unam grandem in ma
nu priore unam in utrisq̃ mammis singulas
obscuras in lumbo interiore unam in utrisque
genibus singulas indextro crure unam. In utris
que pedibus singulas. Omnino est stellarum qua
tuordecim. Effusio aquæ cum ipso aquario est
stellarum xxx. sed in his omnibus prima &
nouissima clara.

Pisces. rorum alter notius alter boreus appella
tur: ideo q̃ unus eorum qui boreus dicitur inter
æquinoctialem &æstuum circulum sub andro
medæ brachio Collocatus &arcticum polum
spectans Constituitur. Alter &est in Zodiaco

be found wound around the north celestial pole. It is one of those northern sky constellations that remains above the horizon and so visible throughout the year to observers in the northern hemisphere. In medieval maps Draco would be depicted as a fierce mythical dragon. Artists of later maps followed the positions of the stars more closely, and therefore depicted Draco as a large-headed snake-dragon.

The dragon is closely linked with the immortal Hercules, who lies next to it in the sky. One of Hercules' twelve tasks was to take golden apples from the garden of Hera on Mount Atlas. The tree that grew such special apples had been a present to Hera on her marriage to Zeus. A dragon was set to guard the tree from unwelcome visitors. But Hercules killed the dragon with poisoned arrows and stole the apples. The dragon was then placed in the sky by Hera.

Planispheric astrolabe
by Muhammad Mahdî al-Khâdim al-Yazî, 1659–1660.
Diameter 7.25 in, gilt brass.

Long before printing made possible the production of star maps or atlases, the planispheric astrolabe served as one of the astronomer's chief aids. An astrolabe is a model of the spherical heavens reproduced on a flat surface. Its main purpose is to show the positions of the heavenly bodies at a chosen time or date as seen from a particular latitude on Earth. It can also be used to solve problems on the positions of the Sun and certain other stars, as well as allowing some observation.

The astrolabe was probably a Greek invention, from around the second century BC; Ptolemy seems to have been acquainted with it. The Arabs learnt of it and brought it to western Europe through their conquest of Spain in the ninth century.

The example here is of a Persian astrolabe dating from the middle of the 17th century. The earliest extant Islamic models, from the tenth century, and those produced by European makers, are of the same basic design. The image on the left presents the front of the instrument. The skeletal brass disc, known as the rete, is a star map. The centre of the rete represents the north celestial pole; its outer edge stands for the Tropic of Capricorn. The solid circle of metal placed off centre represents the ecliptic (the path of the Sun), which is divided into the twelve zodiac signs. The ends of the leaf-type pointers that comprise the rete indicate the positions of

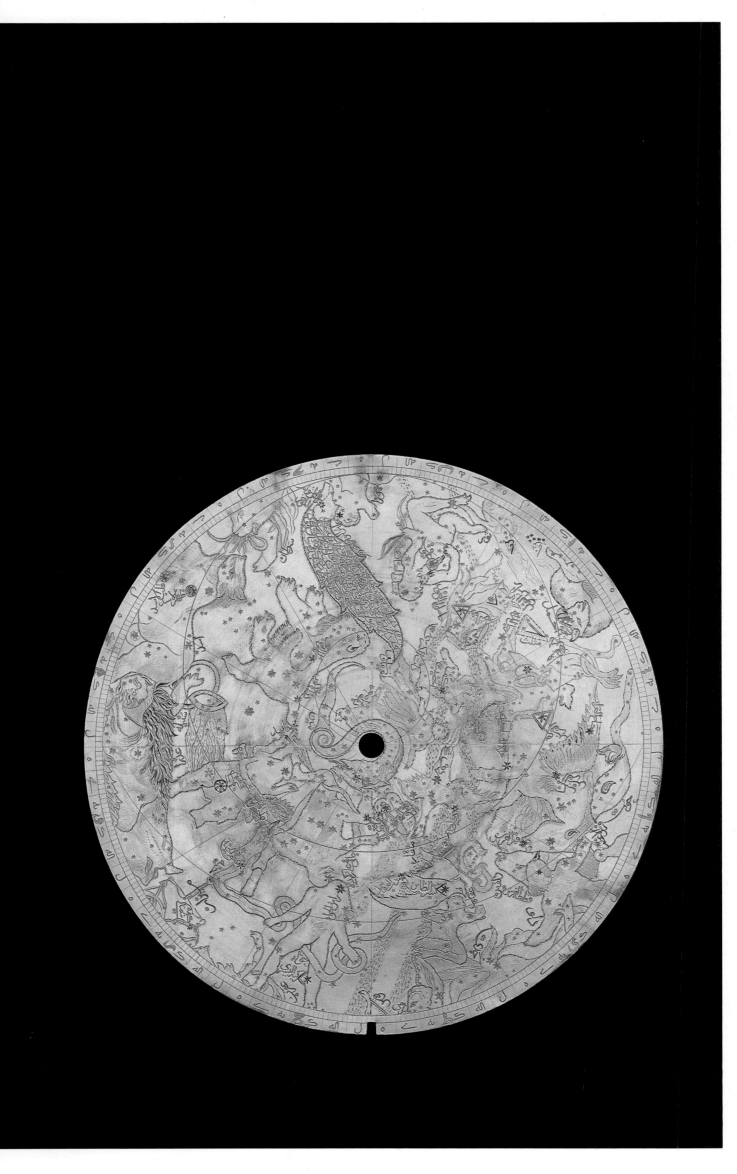

particular stars. Forty-nine stars are identified in this way on this example. Their names are inscribed close by. The rete, used in conjunction with the appropriate latitude plate placed beneath it, would be rotated about the celestial axis to provide a picture of the heavens for a chosen time from a particular place on Earth.

This astrolabe is unique in that it includes a secondary star map showing the northern hemisphere constellation figures. This is displayed on the right. Familiar constellation figures, individual stars and the path of the Milky Way are all included on the map.

*The zodiacal
constellations*
*from British Library
Manuscript Harley 4940
(folio 32). Detail from plate
size 10 × 13 in.*

The twelve zodiacal
constellations are important
providing as they do a
backdrop against which the
movement of the Sun, the
Moon and the planets can be
measured. In particular, they
allow us to keep track of the
Sun quite easily, and so to
chart the progress of the
year; at the same time they
provide us with information
for agricultural, religious and
astrological purposes.

The band of sky
incorporating the zodiacal
constellations is centred on
the ecliptic, the path of the
Sun. It extends to a width of
about nine degrees on either
side of the ecliptic. The Sun
completes one circuit of this
path each year. The
constellations through
which the Sun travels are:
Aries, Taurus, Gemini,
Cancer, Leo, Virgo, Libra,
Scorpius, Sagittarius,
Capricornus, Aquarius and
Pisces. Each of the
constellations occupies a
zone of sky 30 degrees long;
the Sun passing through one
of these zones each month.
Certain positions of the Sun
along its path have particular
significance. The vernal
equinox is the point at
which the Sun moves from
the south to the north of the
celestial equator; day and
night are then equal in
length. The Sun reaches the
vernal equinox on, or about,
March 21 each year. Another
name for this position is the
First Point of Aries; this
stems from the fact that
when this point was defined
as long ago as the second

century BC it was then in the constellation of Aries. Due to precession the vernal equinox is now in the constellation of Pisces. 'Precession' means that the Earth, as it spins, behaves like a dying top, its axis describing, over a very long period of time, a small circle in the sky.

The point at which the Sun travels back to the south of the celestial equator is the autumnal equinox which occurs six months later, on or about 21 September, when once again day and night assume equal length.

The twelve divisions of the zodiac seem to have been established by the first millenium BC. Conspicuous constellations, such as Taurus, at the turn of spring, or Leo, prominent in the mid-winter sky, are believed to be older; they were well recognised as early as 3500 BC. The most recently established zodiacal constellation is Libra, the scales (see p 32). The term 'zodiac' stems from the Greek for animal, for the zodiac is a circle of animals, with the one exception of the sign of Libra.

***The zodiacal
constellations of Gemini
and Cancer***
*from British Library
Manuscript Arundel 66,
(folio 39v), c.1490. Average
image size 4.25 × 4 in.*

Manuscript translations of
Ptolemy's *Almagest* star
catalogue were still being
produced 1,500 years after
the original had first
appeared. These illustrations
are taken from a manuscript
copy prepared around 1490;
it was produced in Latin,
translated from an Arabic
copy which in turn had been
translated from the original
Greek. The manuscript
includes 42 illuminated
constellation drawings. The
figures appear among tables
providing stellar information
such as the latitude and
longitude of stars and an
indication of their relative
brightness.

The two young men
Castor and Pollux (or, more
properly in Greek,
Polydeuces) are the twins of
the constellation Gemini. As
twins they looked alike, and
had the same mother, Leda,
but Pollux was said to have
been fathered by Zeus and
was thus immortal, whereas
Castor was the son of
Tyndareus and therefore
mortal. When Castor died,
Zeus placed him in the sky
with his brother to share his
immortality – the two bright
stars named Castor and
Pollux mark their heads. The
two young men can also be
identified as two other sons
of Zeus – Apollo and

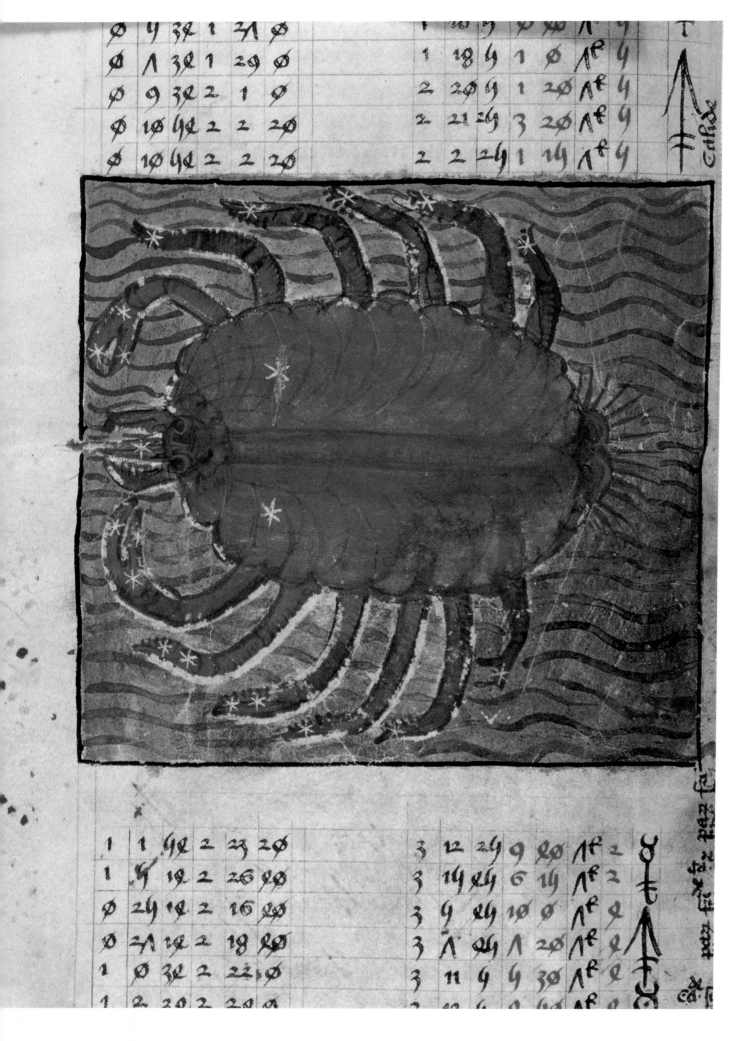

Heracles (the Greek name for Hercules). Later maps show them holding appropriate symbols: a lyre and an arrow for Apollo and a club for Heracles.

Cancer, the crab, was placed in the sky by the goddess Hera. The creature features in the story of the second of the labours of Hercules. As Hercules fought the Hydra – the multi-headed water-snake monster – the crab bit him in the foot. Hercules reacted by stamping on the crab, crushing it.

***The zodiacal
constellations of Leo and
Virgo***
*from British Library
Manuscript Arundel 66,
(folio 40), c.1490. Average
image size 4.25 × 4 in.*

A lion's form can easily be
spotted in the group of stars
that make up the
constellation of Leo. This is
one of the constellations
where the stars most closely
correspond with the figure
formed around them. Four
bright stars mark the limits
of the lion's body, while
others form the curve of its
head; but this relationship is
not so obvious here. As with
all the drawings in this
manuscript, the stars are
placed artistically within the
constellation, rather than the
other way round. The
dominant star which marks
the lion's heart, however, is
undoubtedly Regulus, the
brightest star in the
constellation. The second

brightest marks the lion's tail. Leo featured in the first of the labours of Hercules. On Earth, Leo was the ravaging ferocious lion of Nemea, feared by the whole area. Hercules killed him and used the lion's own claws to strip its pelt, which he wore himself.

There are a number of contenders for the role of Virgo, the virgin. Hyginus identified her as Tyche, the goddess of fortune, who holds a horn of plenty. Or perhaps she is Demeter, the corn goddess, sister of Zeus – in some illustrations she is shown holding an ear of wheat. More usually Virgo is seen as Dike, goddess of justice. She lived on Earth at a time of peace and prosperity, but this was not to last. As mankind turned towards a life of violence and degradation, Virgo retired from the Earth, returning to the heavens.

The northern sky
*from a manuscript text by
Giovanni Cinico, Naples,
1469. Diameter c.4.5 in.*

This charming manuscript
map was included in an
astronomical manuscript
written by Giovanni Cinico
in 1469. It features the
Ptolemaic constellations of
the northern hemisphere.
Ursa Major and Ursa Minor
can be seen back-to-back in
the centre. The zodiac
constellations appear
towards the edge of the map.
At right a roaring lion, Leo, is
chasing a very curious crab,
Cancer. Close by are the
twins, Gemini, who seem to
be sitting on top of Taurus,
the bull.

The map is visually
appealing but of little
scientific value: the positions
of these constellation figures
bear only a slight
resemblance to their true
positions in the sky. This
becomes immediately
obvious when we look at the
two bears in the centre of
the map. In reality the Great
Bear is much larger than the
smaller one; they are both
on the same side of the
north celestial pole, and only
the tail of Draco, the dragon,
comes between them.
Furthermore there is no
attempt either to represent
individual stars or to use a
coordinate system on the
map shown here.

It was during the
following century that the
star map was truly born. In
the first printed star maps,
produced by Albrecht Dürer
in 1515, great care was taken
in positioning the stars, and
coordinates were given (see
page 7). Alessandro
Piccolomini's publication
Stelle Fisse, of 1540, was the
first printed collection of star

maps, as opposed to constellation drawings (see page 10). Individual stars on his maps were identified by consecutive letters, where 'A' signified the most important star. This innovative technique was used by Johann Bayer in his important star atlas of 1603, and foreshadowed the method of star identification we use today.

Towards the close of the sixteenth century, Giovanni Paolo Gallucci produced the first star atlas from which stellar coordinates could be read. His *Theatrum Mundi, et Temporis* of 1588 consisted of woodcut maps of the forty eight Ptolemaic constellations. Lines of latitude and longitude were provided at the edges of the star maps (see page 9).

The zodiacal constellations of Libra and Scorpius
from British Library Manuscript Arundel 66 (folio 41), c.1490. Average image size 4.25 × 4 in.

The faint constellation of Libra, the scales, lies between the constellations of Virgo and Scorpius. The Sun passes through this constellation during November. However, this part of the sky was not always designated Libra: it was at one time part of the adjacent constellation of Scorpius, occupying the area of the scorpion's claws. The Greeks referred to this area as Chelae, the claws, and Ptolemy described the constellation both as Chelae and as Libra. It is difficult to establish who first introduced the constellation of Libra. One conjecture is that it originated with the Sumerians, who, around 2000 BC, referred to the constellation as 'the balance of heaven'.

Libra is usually depicted simply as scales, but the scales are sometimes held by the goddess of justice – Dike, also known as Astraeia – who is depicted in the neighbouring constellation of Virgo. Today, Libra's two brightest stars are a reminder of the constellation's past. The stars, one in each of the scale's pans, are called Zubenelgenubi and Zubeneschamali, meaning the southern and northern claws respectively.

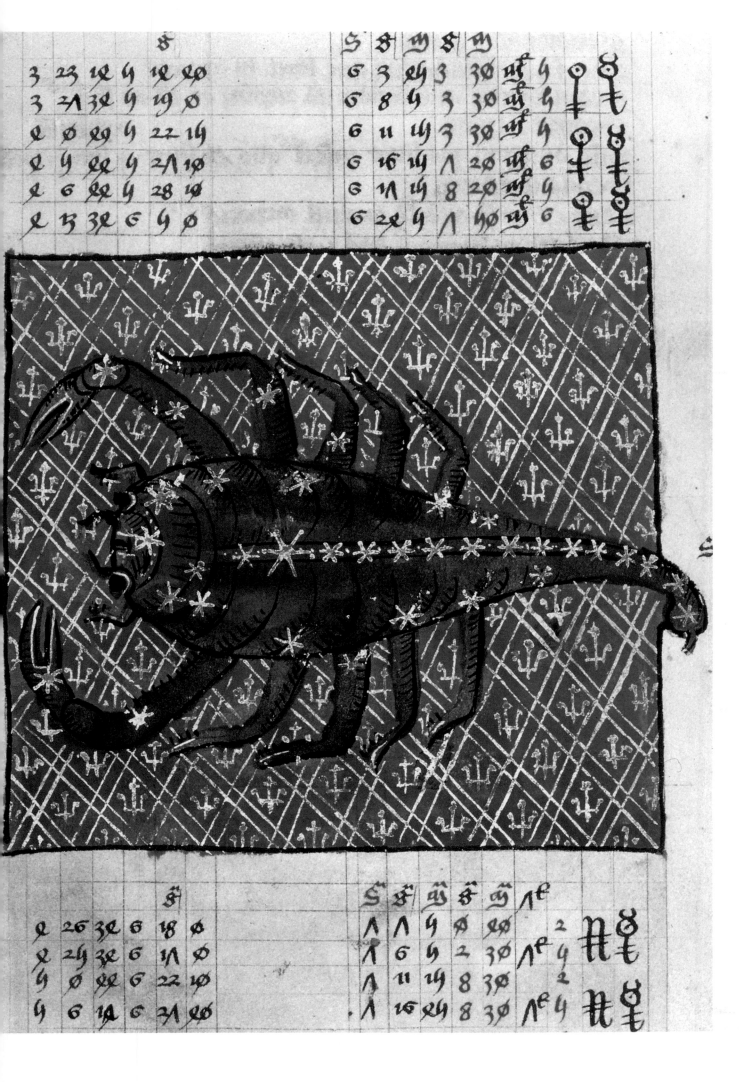

Scorpius is a beautiful constellation to observe, although this illustration does not accurately reflect the positions of the stars in the sky. Nevertheless, the outline of a scorpion can be drawn around the stars. The bright star Antares marks the 'heart' of the creature. Its name means 'the rival of Mars', and its red colouring is just discernible in the night sky. Other stars provide the sting of the scorpion's tail.

The zodiacal constellations of Scorpius, Sagittarius, Capricornus, Aquarius and Pisces
from British Library Manuscript Harley 4940 (folios 31 and 31v). Plate size 10 × 13 in.

The three zodiacal constellations depicted on the left are Scorpius, Sagittarius and Capricornus. Sagittarius, the archer, is one of two centaurs represented in the heavens. He has the body of a horse with the chest and head of a man. In his hands he holds a bow, with an arrow poised ready for flight. The figure of Sagittarius can be identified with Crotus, who is credited with inventing archery, and pursued his sport on horseback. He lived with the Muses, nine daughters of Zeus; at their request, Zeus placed the archer in the sky.

Sagittarius' bow and arrow point in the direction of neighbouring Scorpius, which originally occupied a greater part of the zodiacal band than it does today. The sky once occupied by the scorpion's claws is now filled by Libra. The myth of the scorpion involves the constellation of Orion, the hunter, whom Scorpius stung to death. Quite why it did so is not certain: the alternative theories are that the scorpion was sent on its task either by Artemis, the goddess of hunting, who did not welcome Orion's attentions, or by Earth,

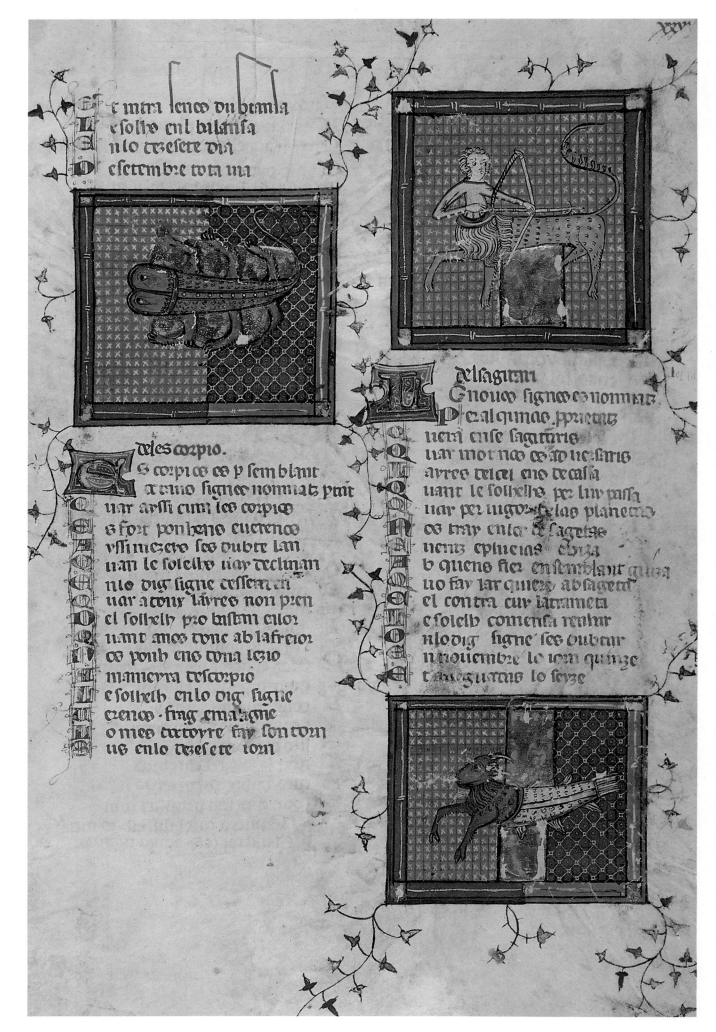

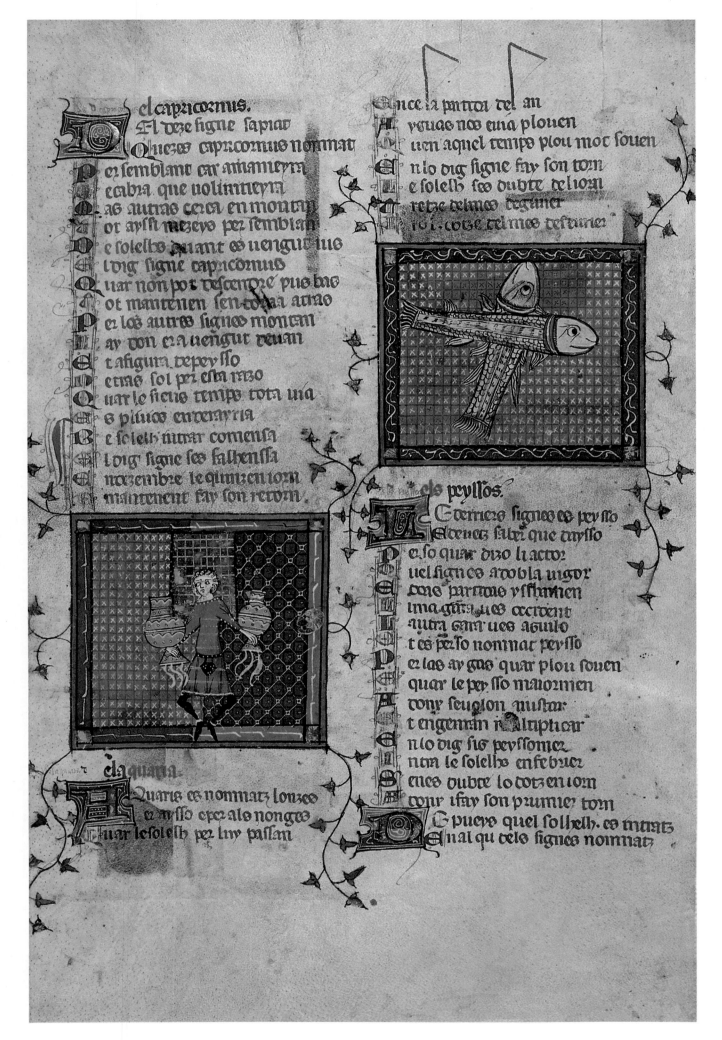

el capricornus.

Once la partida del an

because Orion had boasted that he could kill any creature on Earth.

Placed to the rear of Sagittarius is another strange creature, Capricornus, the sea goat. It has the head and half the body of a goat with the tail of a fish. This constellation is identified with the god Pan, who on Earth had the horns and legs of a goat. Pan was the father of Crotus, and was placed in the sky by Zeus in recognition of his help in battle.

The constellations of Aquarius and Pisces are discussed on pages 36 and 38 respectively.

els peyssos.

el aquaria.

The zodiacal constellations of Aquarius and Sagittarius from British Library Manuscript Harley 2506 (folios 38v and 39v). Image size approximately 4 × 5 in.

Aquarius, the water-bearer, is a difficult constellation to identify in the sky. It has no particularly bright stars and no really obvious pattern. A group of the brighter stars is used as the basis for the water-bearer's jug, and his body is loosely drawn around the remaining stars. In many of the early manuscript drawings, the pictures of the constellations would bear little relation to the stars in the sky, and this depiction of Aquarius is very stylized. The contents of the jug or cup are drawn around a row of stars which does not obviously correspond to anything in the sky.

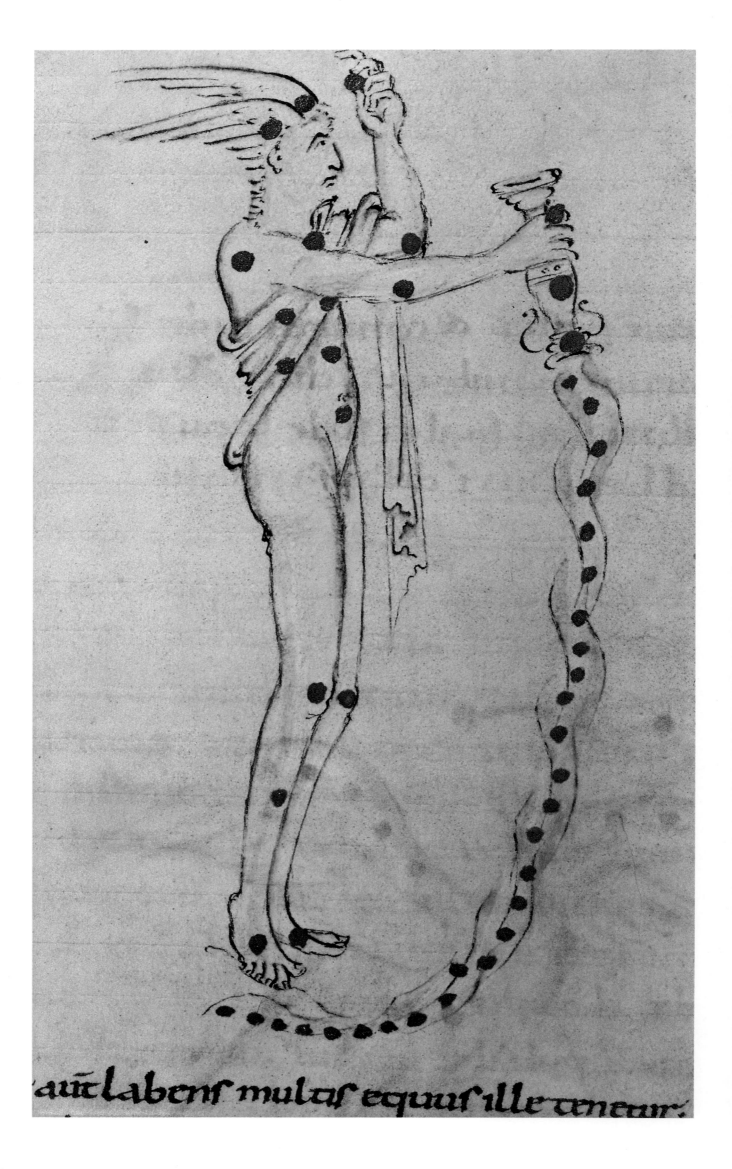

aut labens mulaf equuf ille teneair.

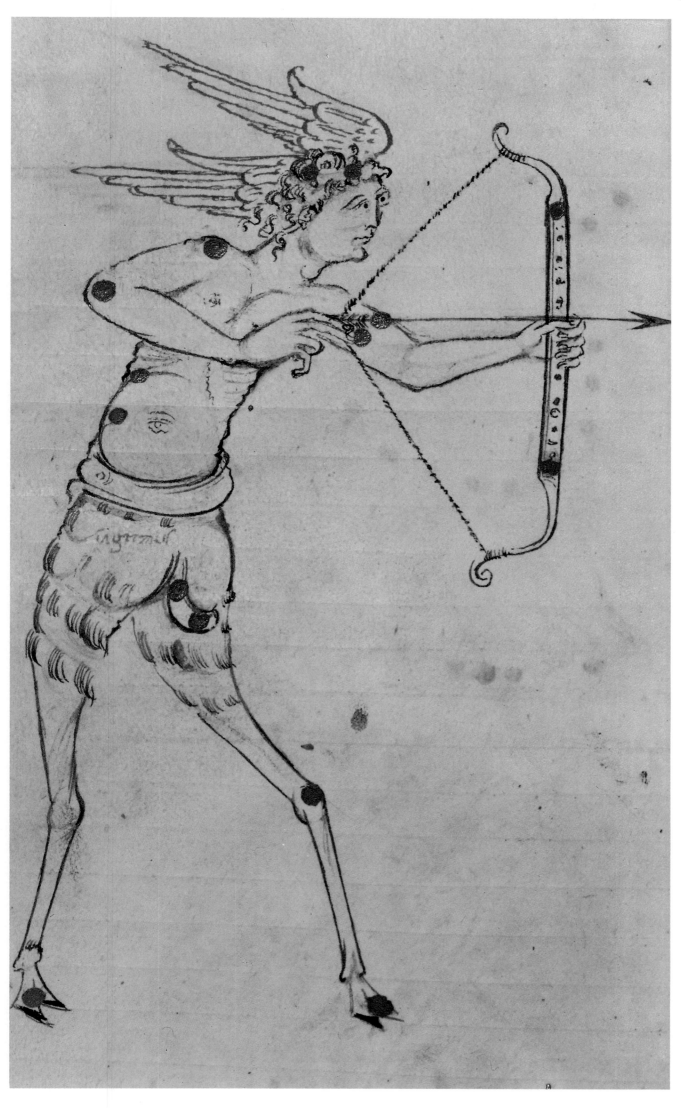

In later maps it is difficult to distinguish the sex of Aquarius. This may be due to one of the stories behind his persona. Aquarius is usually identified as the beautiful Ganymede. His outstanding good looks drew the attention of Zeus, who disguised himself as an eagle and carried Ganymede away to Olympus. Hera, Zeus' wife, was understandably annoyed but she had to tolerate Ganymede, who remained to serve the gods with nectar from his jug.

Two constellations nearby are associated with Aquarius. Aquila, the eagle, represents the disguise that Zeus adopted to capture Ganymede. The water or nectar from Aquarius' jug flows into the mouth of the southern fish that is the constellation of Piscis Austrinus.

The celestial sky
from Astronomicum
Caesareum *by Petrus
Apianus, Ingolstadt, 1540.
Plate size 12 × 18 in.*

In the year 1540 Petrus
Apianus or Peter Apian, as
he is also known, produced a
spectacular book entitled
Astronomicum Caesareum. It
was a celebration of
Ptolemaic astronomy
designed for the Emperor
Charles V and his brother
Ferdinand. The book was so
well received that Apianus,
then Professor of
Mathematics at the
University of Ingolstadt, rose
to the rank of hereditary
nobility soon after its
publication. Today it is
hailed as a triumph, not so
much for its astronomical or
astrological content but
rather as a pinnacle of the
bookmaker's art.

The plate reproduced here
shows the celestial sky most
familiar to western
astronomers of the time. It is
the northern sky, visible
from all European countries.
The southern sky, only
visible from more southerly
latitudes, had not yet been
catalogued and, although
some of the known stars had
been formed into
constellations, it was not
until the next century that
the southern sky was
regularly included in
astronomical publications.

The central constellations
on this star map are shown
in the familiar guise of Ursa
Minor, Draco and Cepheus.
Yet in a planisphere
published in 1533, Apianus
had followed the Bedouin

tradition in which different figures were formed from the stars around the north celestial pole. An old woman and three maidens replaced Ursa Minor; four camels represented Draco, while Cepheus was shown as a shepherd with his sheep and dog. Even though the Bedouin traditions were well known, they were not usually illustrated. Apianus's 1533 planisphere is the only known depiction of these unusual constellations.

Many of the plates in *Astronomicum Caesareum* are suited equally both to astrology and to astronomy. With some effort, the reader can derive planetary positions and other such data required for astrological prediction. Many of the pages are built up with a series of paper volvelles which, when turned and positioned, produce the required data. Every page is hand-coloured, making each copy of the book a unique production. A deluxe edition was further enhanced by gilded stars on the planisphere. The plate reproduced here comes from the less rare standard, but still spectacular, edition. Research has uncovered almost seventy extant copies, and it is believed that in all around one hundred may have survived.

The zodiacal constellations of Aries and Pisces
from British Library Manuscript Harley 647 (folios 2v and 3v). Image size approximately 5 × 5 in.

These pictures of Aries and Pisces were produced in Italy in the ninth or tenth century. The manuscript book that they come from is based on a translation of the work of Aratus, whose poem, *Phaenomena*, written around 275 BC, contained descriptions of 47 constellations. The translation in this manuscript was made by the Roman writer, Marcus Tullius Cicero, in the first century BC. A total of twenty constellations are illustrated, of which Aries is the first. The constellation figures are filled with extracts from the work of Gaius Julius Hyginus, who had gathered together the Greek star myths in the second century BC. Each illustration has Cicero's translation of Aratus at the bottom of the page.

Aries was a winged ram with a golden fleece who saved the young man

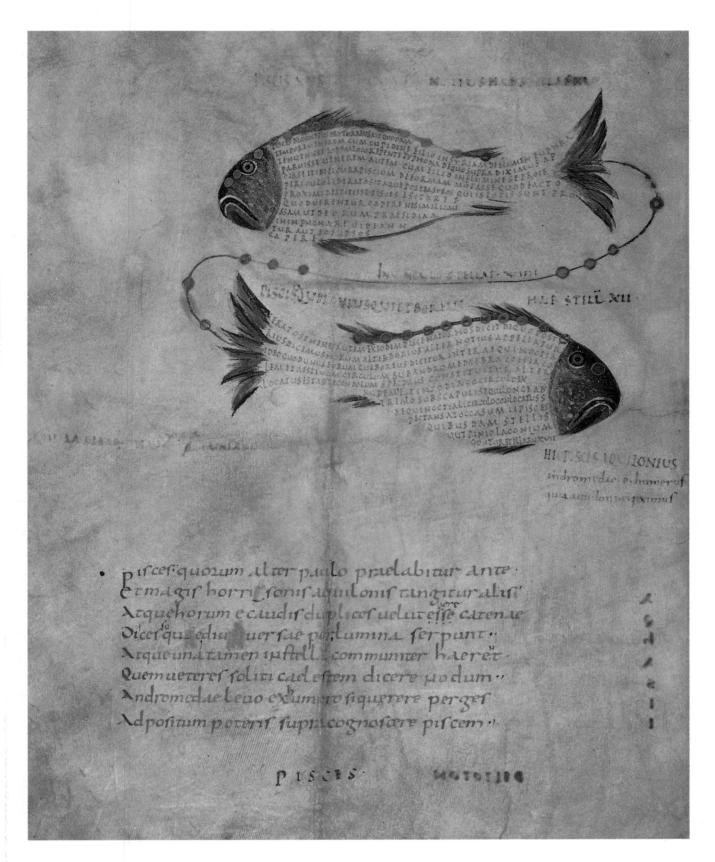

Phrixus from being sacrificed to Zeus. The fleece later became the object behind the voyage of Jason and the Argonauts. If Jason could obtain the fleece, the throne of Iolcus would be his.

There are a number of stories explaining why the two fishes appear in the sky. Hyginus tells of an egg that, having fallen into the river Euphrates, was returned to the land by fishes. Aphrodite was then hatched from the egg and in gratitude to the fishes placed them in the sky. In an alternative story, two fishes rescue Aphrodite and her son, Eros, when their lives are in danger. Both Aries and Pisces are faint but important constellations. In ancient times Aries contained the vernal equinox. This is the point on the celestial sphere where the path of the Sun – the ecliptic – crosses the celestial equator. The Sun reaches this point on or about 21 March each year as it moves northwards. The vernal equinox is now in the constellation of Pisces, due to the effects of precession (see pages pp 6 to 11).

**The zodiacal
constellations of Aries
and Taurus**
*from British Library
manuscript Arundel 66 (folio
39), c. 1490. Average image
size 4.25 × 4 in.*

The story of Taurus is
centred on the god Zeus. The
bull (or, more precisely, half
bull, as only the front of the
animal is represented in the
sky) is in fact Zeus, who took
on this guise to be close to
Poseidon's mortal
granddaughter Europa. On
seeing the handsome bull,
she approached him and sat
on his back. The bull then
waded into the sea,
venturing so far from shore
that Europa had to cling ever
more tightly to him. On
reaching the island of Crete,
Zeus seduced Europa and
their union produced Minos,
King of Crete.

   Taurus's bright stars and
distinctive shape make it
easy to see in the sky, and it
is a very interesting
constellation to observe. The
bull's face is usually formed
around the V-shaped cluster
of stars called the Hyades,
with its horns stretching out
to two single bright stars.
The brightest star in the
constellation, Aldebaran,
marks one of the bull's eyes.

   A group of over two
hundred stars within the
constellation of Taurus

deserves special mention. It is the Pleiades, or Seven Sisters, and is the brightest star cluster in the sky. We know today that the Pleiades is an open star cluster. The stars were formed around 50 million years ago by condensation of the matter in a gas cloud. The cluster appears as a fuzzy patch of light towards the back of the bull, but six individual stars can be discerned with the naked eye, and seven if the conditions are right. These represent the seven daughters of Atlas and Pleione, who were placed in the heavens by Zeus, to save them from the attentions of Orion. The cluster was well known to the ancient Greeks, is mentioned by Ptolemy and Hyginus, and appears in some medieval manuscripts depicted as seven maidens.

Celestial globe
attributed to Thomas Wright, early 18th century. National Maritime Museum, London. Diameter 14.3 in.

Today, we are all familiar with the terrestrial globe, but it was its less well-known companion, the celestial globe, that was in fact the first to be produced. Greek texts dating from before Christ refer to its construction and use. Both the Greeks and the Arabs used celestial globes as observational aids. The Arabs introduced them to western Europe through their conquest of Spain in the ninth century. A number of engraved metal globes produced and used by the Arab world exist. The earliest extant western globes date from the first half of the fifteenth century, although it is known that some were produced earlier.

An early method of production was to place parchment gores over a sphere of papier-mâché and plaster. The more popular and widely-used method of printing the information on to the gores was developed in the sixteenth century. Once printed, the gores would fit over the sphere. They would be shaped like the segments of a peeled orange. Copies could then easily be printed from the copper plates leading to an increase in globe production.

The globe illustrated here is exceptional. Each hemisphere consists of alternate strips of brass and copper-alloy, which in turn alternate with the metal strips of the adjoining hemisphere. Once the metals had been assembled to form the sphere, its surface would have been polished and prepared for the cartographic information. This would have been engraved directly onto the globe, a method leaving no room for error. Both this globe and its terrestrial partner are unsigned but they have been attributed to Thomas Wright of London. His skill and craftsmanship in brass led to his appointment as Instrument Maker to the Prince of Wales. King George I and King George II were amongst his long list of clients.

The first copies of Nicolaus Copernicus' book, *De Revolutionibus*, reached him on 24th May 1543, the day he died. In this book that revolutionised astronomy, Copernicus introduced two ideas, both hinted at by the Greeks. The first idea concerned the Earth's rotation; this makes the stars appear to us to spin round our world every day. Copernicus' second idea was even more astounding. He insisted that the sun remains fixed in position and that the Earth orbits around the sun every year. The Greek philosopher, Aristarchus, had proposed this second possibility in the third century BC. But Copernicus's detailed work placed the theory on a solid foundation. It was taken seriously, and within 150 years the sun-centred system had firmly replaced the Ptolemaic Earth-centred view.

This plate from Cellarius's atlas illustrates the sun-centred system outlined by Copernicus. The planets Mercury, Venus, Earth, Mars, Jupiter and Saturn have circular, uniformly spaced orbits around the Sun. Uranus, further out, was not discovered until 1781. Beyond Saturn can be seen the band of zodiacal constellations. Only five satellites were known. The Moon orbits Earth, and the four Galilean satellites circle Jupiter. In this new system, the Earth moved very quickly; this despite the fact

that there was no proof of the Earth's motion until the eighteenth century. It was in 1725, through James Bradley's discovery of the aberration of starlight, that we learnt that the Earth moves nearly 19 miles every second.

Copernicus (seated at lower right) is popularly remembered as the astronomer who laid the foundations of our modern view of the universe.

The Copernican system
from Atlas Coelestis seu
Harmonica Macrocosmica,
by Andreas Cellarius,
Amsterdam, 1661. Plate size
20.75 × 17.5 in.

This schematic view of the
Copernican solar system
concentrates on the
explanation of the Earth's
seasons. Unlike the other
planets, the Earth is shown
much enlarged and is also
depicted four times. On the
left of the map we see the
Earth at the time of the
vernal equinox. This occurs
at the beginning of spring,
around 21 March, and at that
time the length of daylight
equals the length of night-
time. The Sun is at the
border between Pisces and
Aries. The Earth moves
anticlockwise, and the
bottom of the diagram
shows its midsummer
position, with the Sun
between Gemini and Cancer.
The autumnal equinox
appears on the right of the
map, with the winter solstice
(i.e. Midwinter's Day) at the
top. Note that the Earth's
spin axis is not
perpendicular to its orbital
plane but is inclined by an
angle of 23½ degrees.

The four seasons are
marked around the zodiacal
band, and the orbital path of
each of the planets has the
appropriate orbital period
marked next to it. The
values given are Saturn
thirty years, Jupiter twelve
years and Mars two years.

The two figures at the
bottom of the map indicate
the changes that the
Copernican system had
introduced to astronomy.
The blindfolded ignorance of
the Ptolemaic system (left)
has been replaced by the
enlightenment of the new

Copernican ideas. But in 1661 when this illustration was produced, many problems remained. The new Copernican system still did not provide accurate predictions of future planetary positions. Also, there was no explanation as to the exact form of the planetary orbits, nor any theory for the planets' movement. These queries had to wait for the work of Johannes Kepler and Isaac Newton respectively.

The constellations Ursa Major and Ursa Minor *from British Library Manuscript Arundel 6 (folio 33). Plate size, Ursa Major 4 × 2.5 in; plate size, Ursa Minor 4 × 3 in.*

The best-known constellation of the northern sky is undoubtedly Ursa Major, the Great Bear. Not quite so prominent is its little-bear companion, Ursa Minor. These form two of the five major constellations always visible in the northern sky, whatever the time of year (the others are Cassiopeia, Cepheus and Draco). These two delightful illustrations come from a collection of forty-two painted onto vellum. They form an illustrative device in the manuscript, enhancing the text and the tables of figures. The gold stars bear only a passing resemblance to those of the constellations; they provide little helpful information to an astronomer. But illustrations such as these kept the constellation figures alive through the Middle Ages, and provided a direct link between the constellations of Ptolemy and those depicted in the first printed star charts, the precursors of our modern maps today.

Ursa Major and Ursa Minor circle around the north celestial pole. Within one degree of this is the bright star, Polaris, also known as the Pole or North Star, which marks the tip of Ursa Minor's tail. Polaris thus appears to remain still while the other stars circle around it, and can always be found at a northerly altitude equal to the observer's latitude. Consequently, Polaris was an

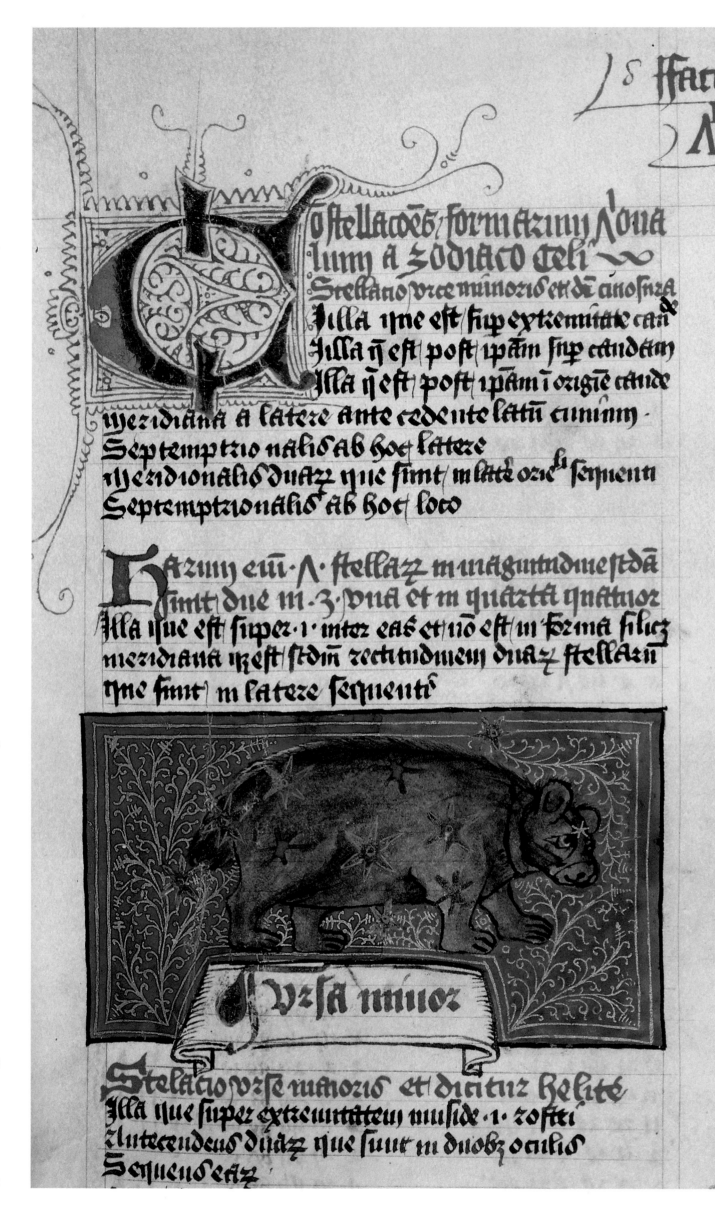

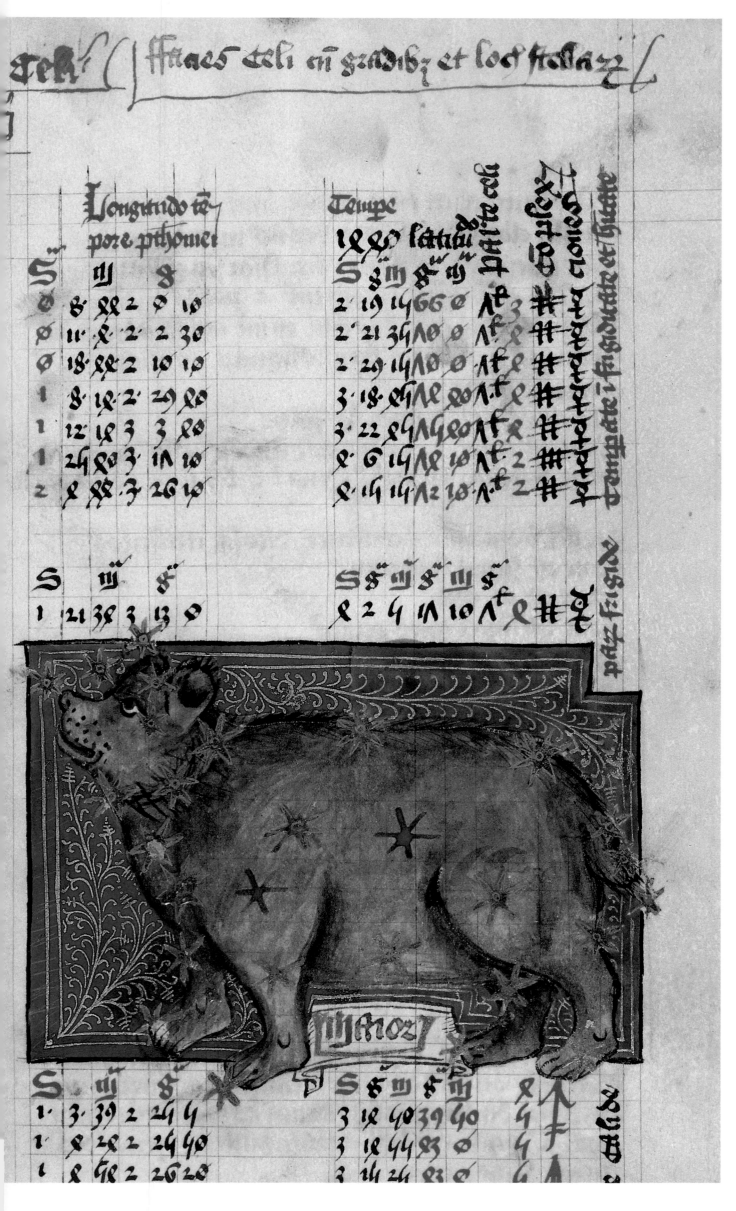

important aid for navigators. Two of the bright stars in Ursa Major point to Polaris. With five others, they form the tail and back of the bear; collectively, they are known as the Plough.

There are a number of stories explaining why the Great Bear is in the heavens. Many such myths feature Callisto: while in the retinue of Artemis, the goddess of hunting, Callisto was seduced by Zeus. When their son was born, Hera, Zeus' wife, attacked Callisto who turned into a bear. Callisto was later carried to the heavens by a whirlwind created by Zeus, and became the constellation of Ursa Major. However, why she and the little bear have long tails is not explained by the mythologists.

***Cygnus and adjacent
constellations***
from Urania's Mirror.
*Published by Samuel Leigh,
London,* c.*1825. National
Maritime Museum, London.
Plate size 8 × 5.5 in.*

Cygnus, the swan, is one of
the most distinctive
constellations of the
northern sky. Five stars
grouped in the shape of a
cross form the basis of the
swan's figure. These stars
can be easily seen in the
night sky; but the cross-
shape is much less obvious
in this illustration. The
bright star, Albireo, marks
the position of the swan's
head, Deneb and Sadr
suggest the body, while the
wings are drawn around
Gienah and the star marked
δ (delta).

Deneb is the brightest star
in the constellation. Along
with two other bright stars,
Altair, in the constellation of
Aquila, and Vega in Lyra
(shown here), Deneb forms a
triangle of bright stars which
dominates the northern sky
in the summer months. Vega
is the fifth brightest star in
the whole sky. The lyre
drawn around it belongs to
the talented musician,
Orpheus. On other star maps
the lyre is superimposed on
an eagle, reflecting the
original meaning of *Vega*
which is thought to come
from the arabic word for
swooping eagle or vulture.

There is more than one
myth associated with many
of the celestial
constellations, and Cygnus is

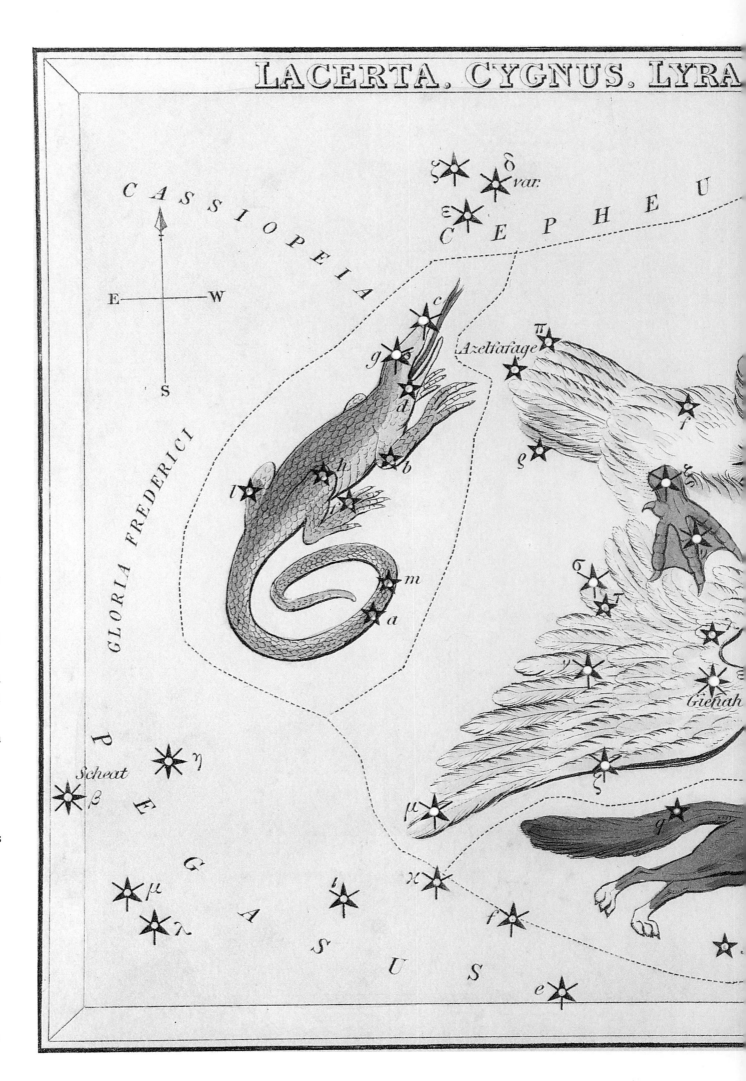

LACERTA, CYGNUS, LYRA

no exception. It is generally accepted that the swan is Zeus in disguise, and that he is courting one of his many loves, but which one? One story links Cygnus with the nearby constellation of Aquila, the eagle. In order to pursue the goddess, Nemesis, Zeus transformed himself into a swan. He persuaded Aphrodite to turn herself into an eagle and pretend to chase the swan, so evoking the pity of Nemesis. Only when it was too late did Nemesis realise that she had been tricked into submitting to Zeus' advances.

Sydney Hall who drew this illustration has used dashed, wavy lines to separate the constellations. The responsibility of defining such boundaries usually fell to the mapmaker. It was not until 1930 that straight-edged, internationally agreed boundaries were included on star maps.

South celestial planisphere

by Thomas Hood. Drawn by Augustin Ryther, and published by Thobie Cooke of London in 1590. Plate size 12 × 12 in.

When Thomas Hood produced his two celestial planispheres in 1590, he seemed as concerned to include background details on the constellations, as to provide astronomical information. Beside each constellation there appears a short commentary on the constellation, its name in various languages, brief mythological details, planetary associations and stellar information.

Hood, the son of a merchant tailor, was a Fellow of Trinity College, Cambridge; he worked from 1588 as a mathematical lecturer in the Leadenhall, London. Hood delivered popular lectures on geometry, astronomy, geography, hydrography and the art of navigation. Some of his lectures were published. In 1590 his

lecture on the use of the celestial globe was published in the form of these two planispheres. Both these star maps, covering the northern and southern hemispheres, would have been very useful as educational aids and as substitutes for the more expensive celestial globe and planispheric astrolabe. Students and others could purchase copies of Hood's planispheres for their own private study from his house in Abchurch Lane, London.

The two planispheres were dedicated to Hood's patron, Lord Lumley (see the coat of arms at upper left) who had first hired Hood in 1587 to lecture privately on the application of mathematics to navigation. These were the first planispheres to be printed in England; together they illustrate the collection of constellations generally accepted before the addition of the newly formed southern sky groupings; these were to come into common use during the course of the next century.

North celestial planisphere

by Thomas Hood. Drawn by Augustin Ryther, and published by Thobie Cooke of London in 1590. Plate size 12 × 12 in.

Hood's northern sky planisphere illustrates the two interesting constellations of Cincinnus and Antinous.

Today we know Cincinnus (centre bottom) as Coma Berenices. Though the group of stars forming this constellation was known to the Greek astronomers, they included it within the boundaries of Leo. Cincinnus did not become a separate constellation until 1551 when the geographer and cartographer, Gerard Mercator of Louvain, included it on a globe. The constellation was quite quickly accepted. This was due in part to the fact that Mercator's globe reached a large number of customers as it was one of the first

globes available with printed paper gores, as compared to the earlier individual manuscript globes. Cincinnus was accepted even more widely when Tycho Brahe included it in his 1602 star catalogue. The hair in the constellation is that of Queen Berenice of Egypt who lived in the third century BC.

Antinous (top right) was also introduced on Mercator's 1551 globe, achieving similar instant popularity. But its reign as a separate constellation was short-lived. Today the stars in this group are included in the constellation of Aquila. On this map Aquila holds Antinous in his claws. Like Queen Berenice, Antinous was a real person: the boy lover of the Roman Emperor, Hadrian. After Antinous's death in AD 130 Hadrian is said to have commemorated his young companion by forming this constellation in the sky.

Tycho Brahe's view of the universe
from Atlas Coelestis seu Harmonica Macrocosmica *by Andreas Cellarius, Amsterdam, 1661. Plate size 20.75 × 17.5 in.*

Tycho Brahe, the Danish astronomer, developed his own view of the universe; this offered an alternative cosmology to that proposed by Nicolaus Copernicus which was at that time gaining popularity. Like the Ptolemaic system, which had served astronomers for 1,400 years, Tycho's system also had a central Earth. The Moon and Sun orbited about the Earth, and the planets – Mercury, Venus, Mars, Jupiter and Saturn – orbited about the Sun. His system was something of a compromise between the old and the new, but gained some followers at the time.

Tycho (shown seated at bottom right) was a very gifted and diligent observer. At his observatory on the island of Hven, in the strait between Denmark and Sweden, he achieved an accuracy of observation that was unprecedented in the history of astronomical measurement. Furthermore he made regular observations of the planets. He looked to his assistant, Johannes Kepler, to apply his observations to verify his view of the cosmos.

Kepler set to work on Tycho's observations of Mars. However, far from proving Tycho's theory to be correct, they proved that he was in fact wrong. They also showed that Copernicus was wrong. Kepler's work revealed that Mars does orbit the Sun and that it does so in an ellipse. This meant

BRAHEVM,
Structura
EX HYPOTHESI
BRAHEI IN
DELINEATA.

that the notion of circular planetary orbits, an idea handed down from the Greeks, was in fact wrong and that uniform planetary motion was also wrong. Mars moved faster when near to the Sun and slower when further away. In this way Kepler developed his first two laws of planetary motion. The third, proposed a few years later, relates the time taken for the completion of one planetary orbit to the average distance from the Sun. Today these three laws still form the basis of our views on planetary motion.

At the close of the sixteenth
century, and at the start of
the following century, the
unformed stars surrounding
the south celestial pole were
observed, catalogued and
grouped into constellations.
A key figure in this work,
and in the subsequent
distribution of information
on globes and charts, was
Petrus Plancius. A Flemish
cartographer and theologian,
Plancius held the post of
mapmaker to the Dutch East
India Company, producing
over one hundred separate
maps in his lieftime.

Plancius recognised the
need to map the uncharted
sky, filling in any gaps with
new constellations. His first
attempts to do so can be
seen on this globe produced
in 1589. Designed by Jacob
and Arnold Van Langren, it
was dedicated to
Christian IV of Denmark,
and is paired with a
terrestrial globe. The stars
depicted were well-known
to navigators, but they had
never been represented in
quite this way before. An
inscription close to the
globe's south pole explains
that the information on the
southern stars and
constellations is based on
the observations of the
explorers, Corsali, Vespucci
and Medina.

This view of the globe
shows the constellation
Triangulus Antarcticus, our
present-day Triangulum
Australei and the two
Magellanic clouds on either

side of it. The Magellanic clouds, although not appreciated at the time, are galaxies, companions to our own Milky Way galaxy. They bear the name of the explorer, Ferdinand Magellan, who first brought them to the notice of European astronomers.

Plancius introduced more constellations on later globes. Three of them – Camelopardalis, Columba and Monoceros – are still in use today. Perhaps of more significance are the twelve created around the south celestial pole; these are depicted overleaf.

The new constellations centred on the South Celestial Pole

from Johannes van Keulen's Boeck zee-Kaardt, *Amsterdam, 1709. Detail of plate size 23 × 19 in.*

The Dutch started ocean-going trade in the closing years of the sixteenth century. The first explorers were to increase greatly the European's knowledge of the southern sky. Two voyages undertaken by Pietr Dirksz Keyser and then Frederick de Houtman were particularly significant. Both made observations of the southern stars. The second voyage which set sail in March 1598 covered a more extended region of the sky than did the first.

The stars observed were formed into twelve new constellations by Petrus Plancius. They appeared for the first time on a globe produced by Jodocus Hondius in 1598, and then on those of other Dutch globemakers.

Johann Bayer's was the first atlas to include the

Cygnius

Andromeda

Triangulum

Aries

Tropicus

Delphinus

Cancri

Pegasus

Æquinoctial

Pisces

Aquarius

Wallevis

Capricornus

Bata Kaitos

Schue

Cetus / Balena

Fomahant

Pisces

Grus

Phenix

Eridanus

Pavo

Indus

Circulus

Toucan

Hydrus

tot Amsterdam Uytgegeven door Cornelis Dan

newly formed constellations. Published in 1603, it is today regarded as one of the finest celestial atlases ever produced, both for its scientific achievement and its artistic style. It contains a considerable number more stars than did previous maps, covering approximately 2,000 in total. Bayer used excellent sources of information on which to base his maps. For the northern stars he referred to Tycho Brahe's catalogue. For the southern constellations, he turned to the work of Keyser, de Houtman and Plancius. The twelve new southern-sky constellations, all of which are still in use today, are: Dorado (a goldfish), Volans (a flying fish), Chamaeleon (a chameleon), Musca (a fly), Triangulum (the triangle), Apus (a bird of paradise), Pavo (a peacock), Indus (the Indian), Hydrus (the lesser water snake), Tucana (a tucan), Grus (a crane) and Phoenix. They are shown in this detail from a celestial sky map in van Keulen's atlas (see pp 66 and 67).

The southern sky

from Atlas Coelestis seu Harmonica Macrocosmica *by Andreas Cellarius, Amsterdam, 1661. Plate size 20.75 × 17.5 in.*

By the time that Cellarius produced his colourful atlas in 1660, the twelve new constellations centred on the south celestial pole were firmly established. They are all illustrated here. The figures that Plancius had used for the constellations were very much symbols of the new and living world, in contrast to the surrounding figures from Greek mythology.

Plancius had been inspired by the discoveries made on the voyages of exploration. Illustrations of the newly found flora and fauna of the southern lands were used to decorate the new maps of those lands. In Plancius's world map of 1594 he included a toucan, a bird of paradise and a chamaeleon.

STELLATUM
ANTIQUUM.

These now appear in the sky as the constellations Tucana, Apus and Chamaeleon, respectively. It is possible that information gathered on the first voyage would have influenced Plancius's choice of constellations. Four of the twelve constellation figures are mentioned in the journals of that voyage. They are Indus, Dorado, Chamaeleon and Piscis Volans.

Exceptions to the New World theme are the figures of Phoenix, Hydrus and Triangulum Australe. Phoenix was the mythical bird reputed to rise, reborn, from its own ashes. Hydrus, the lesser water snake, is a smaller version of Hydra, the largest of all the constellations. Hercules killed Hydra in the second of his labours. The figure of Triangulum Australe repeats the constellation of Triangulum already established in the northern sky by the Greeks.

The celestial sky

from Johannes van Keulen's
Boeck zee-Kaardt,
Amsterdam, 1709. Plate size
23 × 19 in.

Toward the end of the
sixteenth century, a number
of Protestant Flemings fled
to the northern Netherlands
to avoid religious
persecution. They included
the scientist, Petrus Plancius,
and the cartographer,
Jodocus Hondius. Jacob
Floris van Langren, another
cartographer from the
southern Netherlands,
started globe production in
Amsterdam. For the next
fifty years the city became a
centre for innovation and
excellence in the art of
globe-making. Most
prominent amongst the
globe-makers was Willem
Jansz Blaeu.

As a young man Blaeu was
more interested in
mathematics than in the
family herring business. He
studied with Tycho Brahe at
his island observatory before
settling in Amsterdam in

about 1598. Once there, Blaeu started to produce maps, books, globes and atlases. Blaeu's style was popular, and his business flourished. His son Joan, succeeded him, and continued to produce his father's globes. Joan Blaeu created a great world map which included northern and southern celestial planispheres. These were copied and reprinted by Ludovici Vlasblom who identifies himself on the map as a doctor of medicine and a mathematician. The maps were in turn reproduced by the Amsterdam-based cartographer, Johannes van Keulen, who bound them in his sea atlases. It is van Keulen's version which is reproduced here. The southern planisphere at right includes the new constellations which had been introduced just over a hundred years earlier. The Ptolemaic and Copernican systems are included at centre top and bottom.

Celestial globe
*by Jodocus Hondius Junior
and Adriaen Veen, 1613.
National Maritime Museum,
London. Diameter 20.6 in.*

Originally from Flanders,
Jodocus Hondius lived in
London in the 1580s,
working as an engraver and
cartographer. He moved to
Amsterdam in about 1593,
and it was there that he
founded his own publishing
firm, producing maps,
atlases and globes. This was
to become one of the most
important publishing houses
in seventeenth-century
Amsterdam. In 1598
Hondius produced a pair of
globes, the celestial of which
was the work of Petrus
Plancius; this was the first
globe to depict his group of
twelve new constellations.
Plancius had used the
southern sky observations
made by one of his pupils,
Pietr Dirksz Keyser.

When Hondius died, the
business was carried on by
his wife and then by his

sons. In 1613, a year after his death, Jodocus junior collaborated with Adriaen Veen to produce a pair of globes. The celestial globe is shown here. It included the new, now refined, constellations and the older established ones which had been charted using Tycho Brahe's observations. Next to the constellation of Phoenix is a portrait of Tycho Brahe.

The smallest constellation in the entire sky, Crux, was first introduced by Plancius on the globe he created with van Langren in 1589. As new observational data became available, the position of Crux in the sky was to change. From the position taken by the tail of Dorado, it moved to its final, and present, resting place under Centaurus. This, the now accepted, constellation of Crux, first appeared on Hondius's globe of 1598. It can be seen here on his son's globe produced in 1613.

The northern sky

from Atlas Coelestis seu
Harmonica Macrocosmica *by
Andreas Cellarius,
Amsterdam, 1661. Plate size
20.75 × 17.5 in.*

This rather ingenious view
of the northern celestial sky
has the Earth depicted
faintly in the background.
The viewer has the
impression of looking
through the starry sky down
on to the Earth below. Putti
hover in the clouds, holding
banners bearing the title of
the map. Below, groups of
astronomers and their
students discuss astronomy.
They use cross-staffs to
measure the angular
distances between the stars
and then use compass
dividers to place these stellar
positions on to globes.

The map is a perfect
example of the successful
union that took place
between art and
astronomical science during
the Renaissance. Artistic
conservatism was essential
when it came to drawing the
constellations: the principal
outlines of the figures had to
be maintained. The stars in
the tail of the Great Bear
(Ursa Major), for instance,
had to stay in his tail, the
stars in the pans of the
Scales (Libra) had likewise to
stay put, but some variations
of artistic style and figure
interpretations did evolve.
Boötes, the blue-coated
herdsman near the centre of
the map, was at times
presented as a heroic
Renaissance nude. Cellarius,
probably mindful of his own
birthplace in the Palatine of
Germany, and his position as
Rector of the Latin school at
Hoorn in northern Holland,
more sensibly provides him
with a coat, boots and a furry

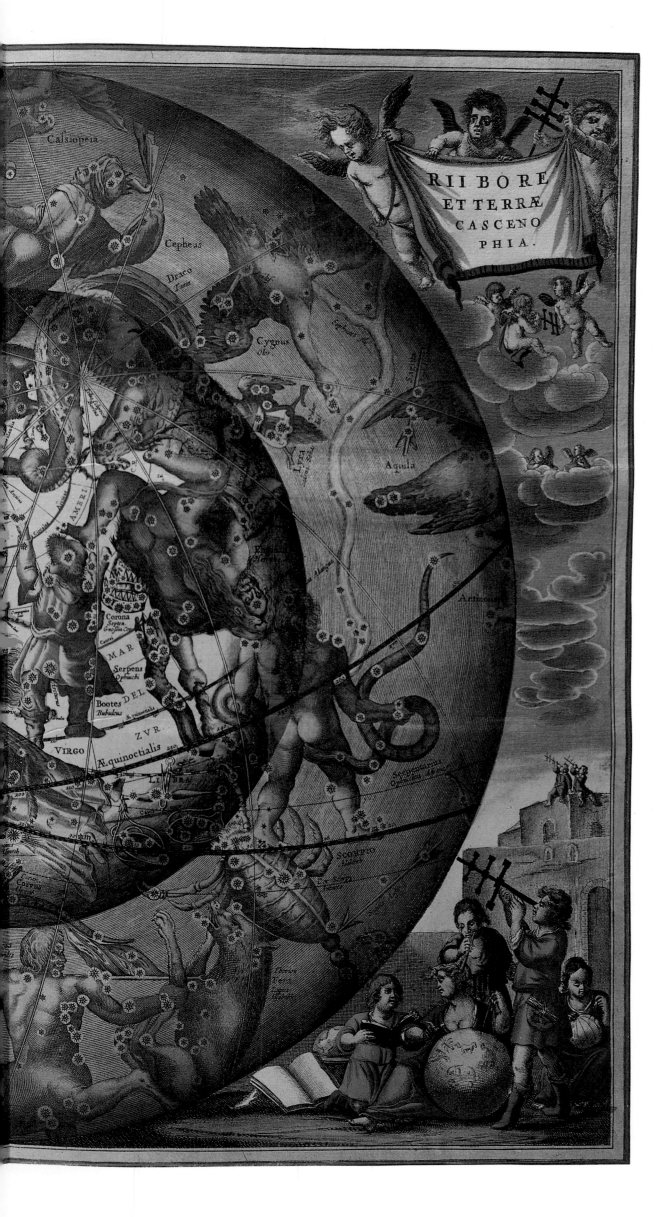

hat – fitting garb for the northern European winter. Cassiopeia, Queen of Ethiopia, seen at the top of the map, fairs less well. She is represented as a buxom, bare-breasted figure, coyly cross-legged and confined to her throne.

One particular problem troubled the artist. Should he represent the figures as seen from Earth (i.e. from the front) or from outside – the more 'divine' view – as seen when looking down on the sky, just as one gazes down on the surface of a globe. In this illustration the figures are seen from behind. Virgo, the Virgin, is shown from the back, and we are treated to the full details of her wings and golden hair.

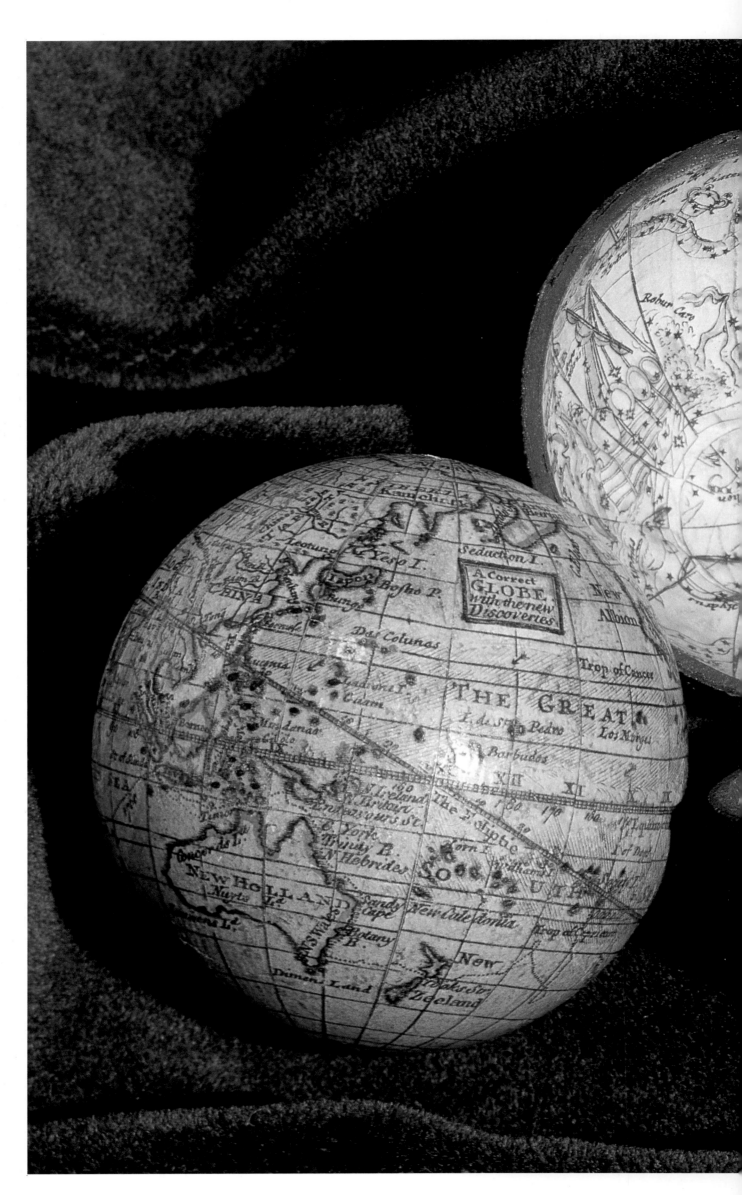

Pocket globe
England, 1772. National Maritime Museum, London. Diameter 2.75 in.

Edmond Halley was still only a young man when he proposed to the Royal Society in London that he should observe the stars in the southern sky and produce a southern sky star catalogue comparable to those for the northern sky.

Accompanied by his friend, James Clark, Halley set sail in November 1676 for the South Atlantic island of St Helena. On arrival they set up an observatory and started their year-long programme of observation. The result was a catalogue of the southern sky which, in terms of accuracy, outstripped those produced by earlier navigators. Without wasting any time, the catalogue was published in late 1678 (although it is dated 1679), along with planispheres of both the northern and southern skies.

Halley's planispheres were copied by map-makers who were keen to incorporate the most accurate and up-to-date information in their work. This pocket globe produced by an unknown Englishman in 1772 incorporates the two celestial spheres within its case. An inscription along the case boasts that it is 'A correct globe with the new constellations [sic] of Dr Halley . . .'. Halley had created a brand new constellation in the southern sky. This was Robur Carolinum, or Charles' oak, which he devised from stars between the constellations of Crux and Argo, close to the south celestial pole.

The oak in the

constellation symbolised the tree in which King Charles II had hidden when fleeing Republican soldiers during the English Civil War. It was a shrewd move by Halley not only to introduce this oak tree, but also to dedicate his southern planisphere to Charles II. Before journeying to St Helena, Halley had been studying at Oxford University, but had left without taking his degree. In December 1678 he was rewarded with a degree, granted by order of the King himself. Even though Halley's constellation was included in the influential atlas of Johann Bode published in 1801, Robur Carolinum has not survived to the present day and it is no longer in the celestial sky.

from Atlas Maritimus *by John Seller, London, 1679. Plate size 19 × 20 in.*

This delightful and unusual chart is the first published map of the zodiacal constellations. In the 1660s, the Royal Society of London considered the need for a reliable map of the zodiac stars, and it was recommended that Fellows of the Society should make the necessary observations. If they did, however, no map was produced. This zodiac map appeared in the following decade, the star positions having been 'Accurately laid down by the said Mr. Edmond Halley'.

In 1678 Edmond Halley had published a star catalogue accompanied by charts of the northern and southern hemispheres. These were the result of a year-long observation programme carried out on the South Atlantic island of St Helena. Halley had been encouraged in his efforts by

ZODIACUS STELLATUS CUJUS LIM VISIBILES VIÆ COMPREHENDUNT

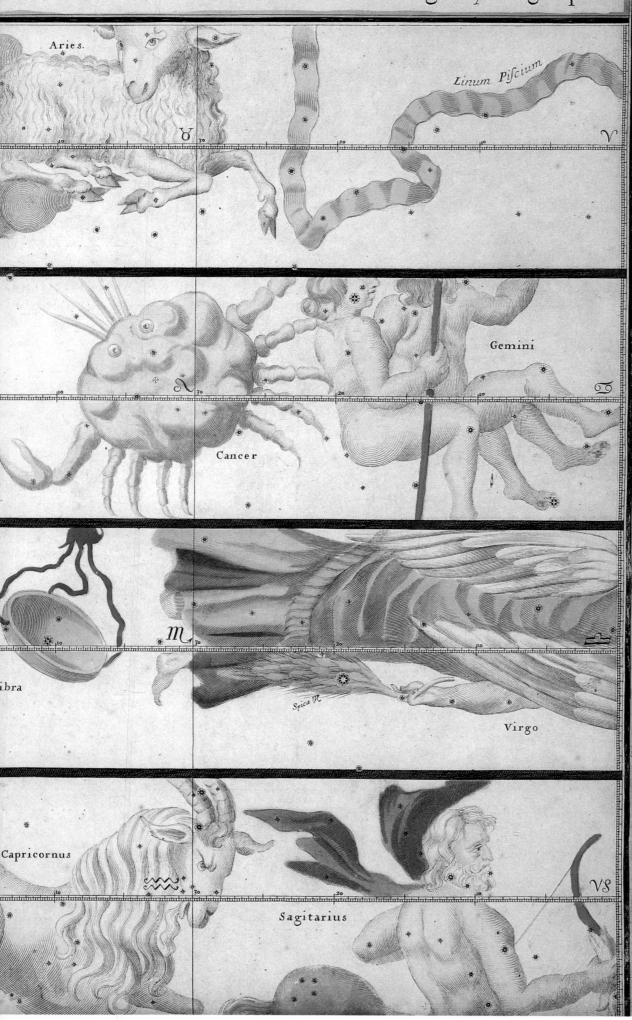

ITIBUS PLANETARUM OMNIUM
JR. Autore Jo: Seller Serenifimi Reg: Hydrographo.

Aries.

Linum Pifcium

Gemini

Cancer

Libra

Spica ℞

Virgo

Capricornus

Sagitarius

the Royal Society, and he was even granted free passage to St Helena by order of King Charles II. Soon after his return Halley was elected a Fellow of the Royal Society. It is possible that the Society's interest in a zodiac map had inspired Halley to produce this one.

The twelve zodiac signs are arranged in four strips which, placed end to end, produce a full zodiac circle centred on the ecliptic, the Sun's yearly path in the sky. The paths of the planets and the Moon all lie within the zodiac band. The advertising claim that this map was 'very useful, at all times, to find out the places of the Planets; wherein may be seen their daily motions' was justified.

The map was bound in a sea atlas published by John Seller, who was Hydrographer to Charles II in the late seventeenth century. From his shops in the heart of London John Seller produced and sold books, atlases and instruments for navigation and surveyance.

The celestial sky
as depicted by Julius Schiller,
from Atlas Coelestis seu
Harmonica Macrocosmica by
Andreas Cellarius,
Amsterdam, 1661. Plate size
20.75 × 17.5 in.

An unusual approach to the
constellations was taken by
Julius Schiller in the early
17th century. Schiller was
not an astronomer but an
Augsburg lawyer with a
strong interest in
cartography. In the year of
his death, 1627, his celestial
atlas, *Coelum Stellatum
Christianum*, was published.

In this work, Schiller
discarded the constellation
figures of mythology
substituting a very individual
and completely new
interpretation of the
heavens. For the northern
hemisphere constellations
he depicted figures from the
New Testament. Cassiopeia
was redefined as Mary
Magdalen (shown here at top
centre). Hercules became the
three magi, and Draco was
depicted as the massacre of
the innocents (at top,
centred on the north
celestial pole). The twelve
signs of the zodiac were
reinterpreted as the twelve
apostles. Shown on this
planisphere are the six
zodiac signs of Sagittarius,
Capricornus, Aquarius,
Pisces, Aries and Taurus.
They are Matthew, Simon,
Judas, Matthew, Peter and
Andrew respectively. The
path of the ecliptic runs from
lower left to upper right. For
the southern hemisphere
stars, Schiller used figures
from the Old Testament:
Centaurus became Abraham
and Isaac, Indus and Pavo
became Jacob (bottom left),
and Hydrus, Tucana and the
Small Magellanic Cloud

STELLATI
ANI HÆMI
POSTERIUS.

became Archangel Raphael (bottom centre). The constellation of Columba, which represents the dove sent by Noah to search for dry land, is the only constellation that remains unaltered (bottom right).

The atlas consisted of fifty-one maps in all, forty-nine of which were centred on the major constellations, and two hemispheres. It did not attract a particularly wide readership, but when Andreas Cellarius republished Schiller's two planispheres in his own atlas later in the century they reached a larger audience. The two Cellarius planispheres are reproduced on both this and the following page.

The celestial sky

*as depicted by Julius Schiller,
from* Atlas Coelestis seu
Harmonica Macrocosmica *by
Andreas Cellarius,
Amsterdam, 1661. Plate size
20.75 × 17.5 in.*

Julius Schiller's celestial
maps were incorporated in
his atlas of 1627, *Coelum
Stellatum Christianum*. His
maps are initially captivating
in their radically alternative
depiction of the
constellations; but their
scientific importance should
not be overlooked. The
representation of the
Christian heavens was not
Schiller's only motive in
producing his atlas. Schiller
had collaborated with
another Augsburg lawyer,
Johann Bayer, and an
Augsburg doctor, Raymond
Minderer in planning a new
celestial atlas with improved
star positions. The outcome
was, in essence, a revision of
Bayer's own celestial atlas,
Uranometria, published in
1603. The new atlas would
incorporate the most
accurate and wide-reaching

STELLATI ANI HÆ RIUM PRIUS.

of astronomical observations available.

Schiller's atlas was perhaps the best collection of celestial maps available at that time, until Johannes Hevelius published his work sixty years later. It was Bayer who carried out much of the astronomical work for the maps while Schiller prepared the constellation figures. The figures were then drawn by Johann Mathias Kager, while Lucas Kilian engraved them. Others joined in at various stages to produce a work of many hands.

On this, the second of Schiller's planispheres which was reproduced by Cellarius in his atlas of 1661, the zodiacal constellations, centred on the ecliptic, run from upper left to lower right. Gemini, Cancer, Leo, Virgo, Libra and Scorpius are replaced by Schiller's new constellations of Jacob, John, Thomas, Jacob, Philip and Bartholomew. The constellation of Argo Navis is now Noah's ark (lower left).

The constellation of Hercules

as depicted by Julius Schiller,
from Atlas Coelestis seu
Harmonica Macrocosmica *by*
Andreas Cellarius,
Amsterdam, 1661. Detail of
plate size 20.75 × 17.5 in.

The stars that make up the
great mythical hero,
Hercules, were depicted as
the three magi by Julius
Schiller in his Christian
heavens. Schiller's atlas,
produced in monotone,
included 49 plates, dedicated
to the main constellations.
The subject of each plate was
drawn boldly. The other,
adjacent constellations were
ghosted in. This colourful
detail of the three magi is
from Schiller's planisphere
reproduced in Cellarius's
atlas. On the left of the magi
is the constellation of Boötes
depicted here as St Sylvester.
Between them lies Corona
Borealis, the bejewelled
crown of Princess Ariadne of
Crete who, according to
mythology, had helped

STELLATI
ANI HÆ
RIUM PRIUS.

Definitor

Ser

Colurus

cus Æstinus Solstiti:

S. Benedictus
cum Spiris Eiusd.
Al Serpentarius
cum Serpente.

Theseus slay her half-brother, the Minotaur. In Schiller's sky the crown is now one of thorns, worn by Christ on the cross.

Schiller interpreted other astronomical objects as Christian figures. The Sun was to become Christ, the Moon, the Virgin Mary, while the planets Mercury, Venus, Mars, Jupiter and Saturn were identified as St Elias, John the Baptist, St Joshua, Moses and Adam, respectively.

Schiller's was the only attempt to Christianise the heavens so completely, but others introduced biblical constellations that had more lasting appeal. Noah's dove, Columba, and the cross, Crux, are obvious examples. They were accepted by the astronomical community and both are in use today, as are Camelopardalis, ridden by Rebecca as she travelled to Canaan, and Monoceros, the unicorn, which is mentioned in the Old Testament.

The northern celestial and terrestrial planispheres

from A Tutor to Astronomy and Geography *by Joseph Moxon, London 1674. Image size 22 × 18.5 in.*

Joseph Moxon, a Yorkshireman by birth, ran a successful business in London, producing and selling scientific instruments, books and maps. He became Hydrographer to King Charles II in 1670, and eight years later he was elected a Fellow of the Royal Society. He had a number of London shops which all traded under 'the Sign of Atlas'; the first was in Cornhill, followed by others in Great Russell Street, Ludgate Hill and Warwick Lane. In 1694 he was also selling his goods by the Parliament Stairs in Westminster Hall, London.

Moxon lived in the Netherlands for a number of years when he was in his early teens. On a return visit in 1652 he stayed in Amsterdam. While there he studied with the cartographer Joan Blaeu. His translation of some of Blaeu's work was published in 1654 as *A tutor to Astronomy and Geography, or, an easie and speedy way to understand the Use of both the Globes, Celestial and Terrestrial.* Moxon rewrote and reissued the work in 1659. This illustration has

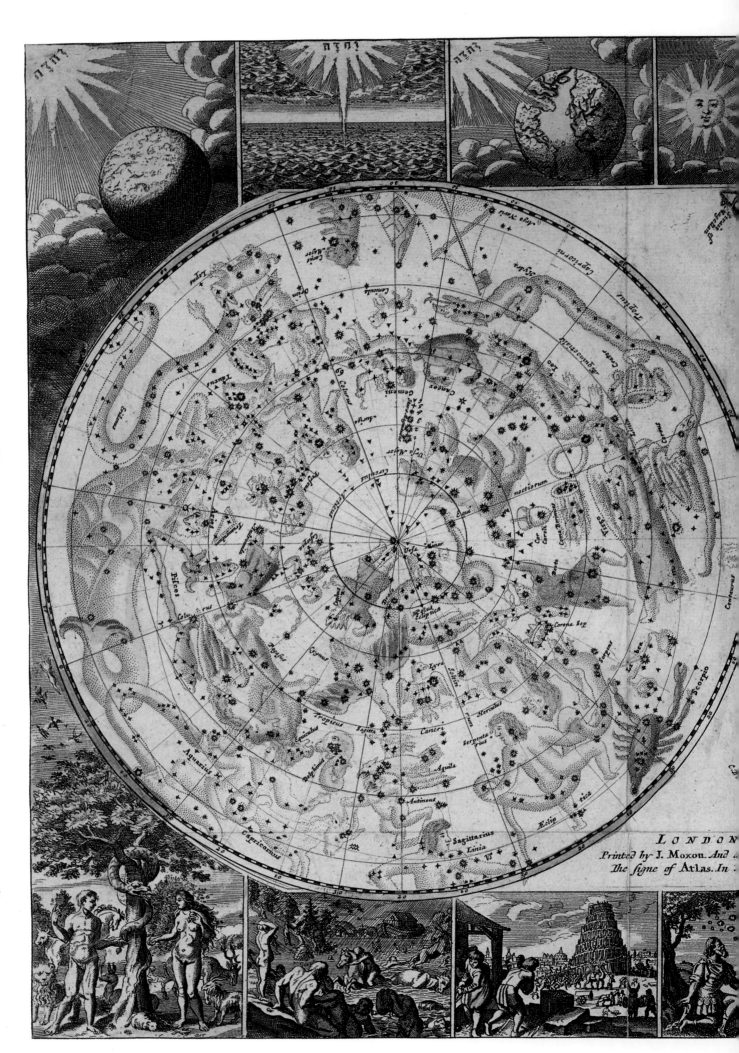

been taken from the third edition of 1674.

On the left is the northern celestial planisphere, with lightly drawn constellation figures. Moxon stippled these figures, engraving them with small dots rather than lines. He stated in the text that he had included the constellation figures because they were convenient, but he went on to explain that 'they must be . . . faintly and simply expres'd' because deep shadows and unnecessary flourishes would cause distraction and the stars would be less conspicuous.

The northern celestial planisphere is accompanied by a northern terrestrial planisphere. They are surrounded by scenes from the Old and New Testaments.

The northern sky
by Carel Allard, Amsterdam,
c.1700. National Maritime
Museum, London. Plate size
24.75 × 21.5 in.

The two maps on this and
the following page were
produced by the Dutch
mapmaker and publisher,
Carel Allard. He inherited
the family business on the
death of his father in 1691,
and Carel's two sons in turn
were to follow him into the
map trade. Working from a
shop in Amsterdam, Allard
produced many maps and
some atlases which were
compilations of the best
contemporary maps. The
two maps reproduced here
are single sheet maps; they
can also be found in Nicholas
Visscher's *Atlas Minor* of
1717 and Georges Sanson's
Atlas Nouveau of 1727. Like
all coloured maps of this
period, these would have
first been produced in black
and white, and then
individually water-coloured.

On this page the central,
dominant map shows the
northern celestial sky. The
constellations are the
traditional Ptolemaic ones
with a few exceptions.
Notable deviations are Coma
Berenices, Camelopardalis,
and the two rivers, Tigris
Fluvius and Fluvius
Jordanus. Some of the
constellations are given
more than just their names;
Cepheus and Cassiopeia are
described as the father and
mother of Andromeda,
respectively. The brightness
of an individual star is
indicated by the size of its
symbols on the map. An
account of a constellation is
given in the two tables at
either side of the central
map; these tables list the
number of stars in a

HEMISPHÆRII SEPTENTRIONALIS Stellæ.

Magnitudines	Prima	Secunda	Tertia	Quarta	Quinta	Sexta	Nihil	Summa
Ursa Minor	0	2	1	5	3	8	0	19
Ursa Major	0	6	4	13	7	9	0	39
Draco	0	1	13	13	10	1	0	38
Cepheus	0	0	3	10	9	12	0	34
Camelopardalus	0	0	0	2	6	21	0	29
Fluvis Iordanis	0	1	1	8	8	12	1	31
Bootes	1	0	6	13	7	12	0	39
Corona Borealis	0	1	0	4	6	9	0	20
Hercules	0	0	10	18	10	24	1	63
Lira	1	0	2	3	6	5	0	17
Fluvius Tigris	0	0	0	16	3	19	0	36
Cygnus	0	1	8	14	2	15	0	40
Sceptrum	0	0	0	1	8	8	0	17
Cassiopea	1	0	4	6	6	20	0	37
Perseus	0	2	4	10	18	11	0	45
Auriga	1	1	0	9	15	20	0	46
Serpentarius	1	0	7	7	6	5	0	26
Serpens Ophiuchi	0	1	8	9	2	24	0	44
Sagitta	0	0	0	3	1	4	0	8
Aquila	0	1	4	1	7	1	6	24
Antinous	0	0	6	1	0	5	0	12
Delphin	0	0	5	0	1	5	0	11
Equuleus	0	0	0	4	0	0	0	4
Pegasus	0	2	3	10	3	7	0	25
Andromeda	0	3	2	9	14	5	0	33
Triangulum	0	0	0	3	2	0	0	5
Lilium	0	0	1	2	4	0	0	7
Coma Berenices	0	0	1	11	1	0	0	13

Zodiaci Constellationes

	Prima	Secunda	Tertia	Quarta	Quinta	Sexta	Nihil	Summa
Aries	0	0	1	3	5	8	0	17
Taurus	0	1	1	1	8	10	0	21
Gemini	0	2	1	2	9	4	0	18
Cancer	0	0	0	1	4	15	1	21
Leo	0	2	7	5	3	8	0	25
Virgo	0	1	6	8	10	14	0	39
Libra	0	2	3	10	7	5	0	27
Scorpio	0	2	0	2	2	1	0	7
Sagittarius	0	0	0	5	1	4	1	11
Capricornus	0	0	3	0	6	8	2	19
Aquarius	0	0	3	5	8	3	0	19
Pisces	0	0	0	5	13	12	0	30
Summa	5	32	118	252	241	364	6	1018

Magnitudines Groote der Sterren	Prime Sec.	Tert.	Quart.	Quint.	Sext.	Neb.	Summa
Stellæ Hem. Septent. Sterren v d. Noorder C.	5 32	118	252	241	364	6	1018
Stellæ Hemisph. Merid. St. v d. Zuid-Cirkel	11 35	109	225	224	157	5	766
Summa	16 67	227	477	465	521	11	1784

Summarium Stellarum, cujuscunque magnitudinis
utriusq; Hemisphærii conficit 1784
De Hoofd som der Sterren in de Noorder en Zuider
Cirkel of Hemels helft is van 1784 Sterren

PLANISPHÆRII COELESTIS H
Calculatum *ad finem* Anni MDCC, *pro* Ævo XVIII præsent
Cum Privilegio Potentissimoru

Variæ Observationes situs Primæ Stellæ tertiæ Magnitudinis in
Timocarides observarunt in Gradu 78 Lat' Bor' et in Gr. 2 o V Ptolomæus 265 annis p
Hipparchus, 150 annis post observavit in Grad 4. o V. Albategnius 740 annis

Proportio Stellarum Fi
Magnitudines ✱ Prime
✱ Tertiæ 20 ad ° 9 ✱ Quarte 3 ad 2
Distant a Terra 12000 ejusdem semi - diametris seu 12

...ultis Stellis auctum et editum a CAROLO ALLARD, Amstelo Batavo,

constellation of a said magnitude. The table on the left relates to the constellations depicted on this page; the one on the right refers to the southern sky map on the following page.

The two circular maps at top left and right are the two celestial hemispheres. Their stars have been grouped together in an alternative constellation system. The figures, animals and objects are all taken from the Christian doctrine. This scheme was put forward by Julius Schiller in 1627. It is discussed on pages 76 and 77 where three of Schiller's maps are reproduced.

HEMISPHÆRII MERIDIONALIS Stellæ

Magnitudines	Primæ	Secundæ	Tertiæ	Quartæ	Quintæ	Sextæ	Nebul.	Summa
Balena	0	2	8	13	5	0	0	28
Serpentarius	0	0	1	3	3	0	0	7
Orion	1	5	3	17	20	16	0	62
Eridanus	1	0	10	29	3	3	0	46
Lepus	0	0	4	4	5	1	0	14
Canis Major	1	1	6	2	9	0	0	19
Columba	0	2	0	5	3	0	0	10
Canis Minor	1	0	1	0	0	9	0	11
Unicornis	0	0	3	10	3	6	0	22
Argo Navis	1	7	8	10	15	2	0	43
Hydra	1	0	3	13	12	20	0	49
Crater	0	0	0	8	1	2	0	11
Corvus	0	0	4	1	5	1	0	11
Crux	0	3	1	0	0	0	0	4
Centaurus	1	4	6	13	10	1	0	35
Lupus	0	0	2	8	10	1	0	21
Ara	0	0	1	6	0	1	0	8
Corona Australis	0	0	0	4	3	5	0	12
Piscis Australis	1	0	3	10	3	0	0	17
Grus	0	0	3	5	3	0	0	13
Phoenix	0	2	4	5	2	3	0	16
Indus	0	0	5	6	3	0	0	12
Pavo	0	1	3	4	2	6	0	16
Apus Indicus	0	0	0	3	9	1	0	13
Musca	0	0	0	0	0	0	0	4
Cameleon	0	0	0	0	7	3	0	10
Triangulum	0	0	1	3	0	0	5	5
Hirundo Marina	0	0	0	0	7	1	0	8
Dorado	0	0	1	2	1	0	0	5
Nubes	0	0	0	0	1	1	0	3
Pica Indica	0	0	4	2	3	0	0	9
Hydra	0	0	2	2	10	0	0	14
Nubecula	0	0	0	1	1	0	1	3
Quadratum	0	0	0	2	0	2	0	4

Zodiaci Constellationes

	Primæ	Secundæ	Tertiæ	Quartæ	Quintæ	Sextæ	Nebul.	Summa
Aries	0	0	0	0	3	0	0	3
Taurus	1	0	3	7	10	10	0	31
Gemini	0	1	3	4	0	6	0	14
Cancer	0	0	2	2	5	11	0	20
Leo	0	0	0	4	5	8	0	17
Virgo	1	0	0	0	3	7	0	11
Libra	0	0	0	0	0	0	0	
Scorpio	1	1	10	0	6	3	3	31
Sagittarius	0	3	8	3	6	1	0	21
Capricornus	0	0	2	1	6	6	0	15
Aquarius	0	0	1	6	15	7	0	29
Pisces	0	0	1	0	5	3	0	9
Summa	11	37	109	224	224	157	5	766

Stellarum Magnitudinum Characteres
Groottens der Sterren

Primæ _____ ✳ De Eerste
Secundæ _____ ✴ De Tweede
Tertiæ _____ ★ De Derde
Quartæ _____ ✦ De Vierde
Quintæ _____ ✧ De Vyfste
Sextæ _____ ⋆ De Sesde
Nebulosæ _____ · De Nevelachtige

...um cum Diametro Terræ

...d 13 ✳ Secundæ 55 ad 18
... Quintæ 50 ad 29 ★ Sexte 15 ad 22
... Milliaribus Germanicis seu deniq: 4850000 Italicis

The southern sky

by Carel Allard, Amsterdam, c.1700. National Maritime Museum, London. Size 24.75 × 21.5 in.

As might be expected of a mapmaker based in Amsterdam, this southern sky map includes the new constellations formed as a result of the observations made by the Dutch navigators one hundred years earlier. In addition to the twelve that Petrus Plancius had introduced in 1598, it depicts two more of his which are now known as Columba and Monoceros. Easily seen, just above the centre of the map, is Columba Noe, the dove sent by Noah to find dry land. It is returning triumphant with a twig in its mouth. Close by, crossed by the path of the Milky Way, is Unicornis al Monoceros, the unicorn.

Surrounding the southern sky map are illustrations of

the planets that were then known by astronomers. The Earth, at left, is shown with part of it experiencing the total solar eclipse of 12 May 1706. The Sun which was then in the constellation of Taurus is obscured by the Moon lying within its light path. Jupiter is shown with four of its satellites. The Italian astronomer, Galileo Galilei, who was the first man to look at Jupiter through a telescope, discovered these four 'Galilean' satellites in 1609. They were later given the names of Callisto, Ganymede, Io and Europa. Close-ups of the Sun and Moon are at top left and right. A key to some of the named lunar features is also given. Unfortunately, some of the other text details have been partially hidden by the blue over-painting of the sky which forms the backdrop of the illustrations.

The celestial sky

from Johannes van Keulen's
Boeck zee-kaardt,
Amsterdam, 1709. Size 23 ×
19 in.

Johannes van Keulen was
the founder of a family firm
that operated for over two
hundred years. The family
were cartographers and
instrument-makers who
published nautical texts on,
for example, ship-building
and maritime law. In 1680
Johannes produced his *Zee
Atlas* which proved to be
very popular; nine editions
being produced within five
years.

The *Boeck zee-kaardt*,
published in 1709, was
produced by Gerard van
Keulen even though it bears
his father's name. It included
seventy-seven coloured
maps and charts, and
nineteen views. The maps
covered Europe, Africa and
America, with details of
European countries,
particularly France, and
views or plans of cities, such

as Amsterdam and Nice. The majority of the maps had been produced by a variety of cartographers, and then simply assembled for this atlas. Two celestial charts were also included: the one shown here and another consisting of northern and southern planispheres (see pages 62 and 63).

This star map which covers the whole of the celestial sky includes the new southern sky constellations formed after the Dutch voyages in the 1590s. However, it is perhaps misleading to use the term 'new' to refer to discoveries made over a century previously. The constellations had become recognised. This map was reissued in atlases produced by other cartographers throughout the course of the eighteenth century. This highlights the fact that few atlases offered anything new, they simply reproduced extant maps.

The constellation of Lynx
from Urania's Mirror.
*Published by Samuel Leigh,
London, c.1825. National
Maritime Museum, London.
Plate size 8 × 5.5 in.*

The astronomer, Johannes
Hevelius, produced an atlas
of 56 maps to accompany his
star catalogue published in
1690. All but two of the
maps were centred on the
major constellations. The
remaining two showed the
stars of the northern and
southern hemispheres.
Hevelius charted the
northern stars according to
his own observations. For
his southern hemisphere
map, he used the
observations of the
astronomer Edmond Halley.

Hevelius introduced nine
new constellations eight of
which are in the northern
sky. The constellation of
Canes Venatici, the two
hunting dogs held by Boötes,
had already been depicted by
cartographers of the
sixteenth century, but only
became more widely used
through Hevelius's work. He
created Lacerta, the lizard,
out of faint stars between
Cygnus and Andromeda; and
the constellation of Lynx he
formed from equally weak
stars between Ursa Major
and Auriga. Hevelius
reflected that one would
need the sharp sight of a
lynx to see the stars in this
constellation. Hevelius was a
particularly gifted observer
with sharp vision who
achieved accurate results
without the use of telescopic
sights on his instruments.

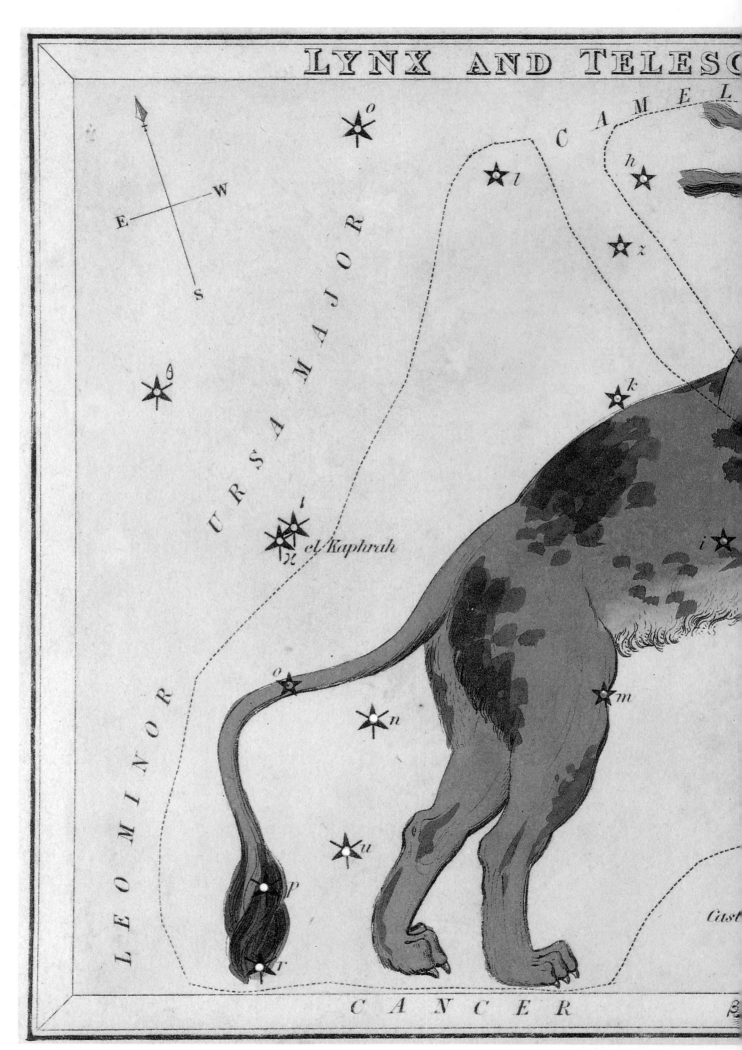

E O P A R D A L I S

a

d

b

δ

A

U

R

Capella vel Alioth

α

Menkalinan

ββ

R

η *ζ*

Duo Haedi

I

d

g

G

θ

A

χ

El Nath *β*

s

θ

Sid.^t Hall, sculp.^t

G E M I N I

Pollux

Another animal, the little lion, Leo Minor, was created from stars close to the bigger version. Vulpecula and Anser, now known simply as Vulpecula, is a fox with a goose in its mouth. Hevelius placed the shield, Scutum Sobiescian, in the sky. It was introduced in honour of King John III Sobiesci of Poland.

All six of these constellations are still in use today. The two which failed to gain popularity are Triangulum Minus, and Cerberus, the mythical three-headed monster that guarded Hades. The southern-sky constellation introduced by Hevelius, is Sextans Uraniae; this is Hevelius's own instrument with which he made the observations for his catalogue. It is still in the sky today, known as Sextans.

The north celestial sky
from Atlas van Zeevaert en
Koophandel Door de
Geheele Weereldt *by Reiner
and Josua Ottens,
Amsterdam, 1745. Plate size
23.5 × 19.5 in.*

The skills of a
mathematician and a first
class cartographer were
combined to produce a
number of astronomical
images in the mid-
eighteenth century. The men
involved were Johann
Gabriel Dopplemayr, a
professor of mathematics in
Nuremberg, and Johann
Baptist Homann, the founder
of the Nuremberg
cartographic publishing
house. In their *Atlas
Coelestis* they produced
thirty plates of astronomical
material. Ten of these are
star charts. Two of them are
reproduced on this and the
following page.

The plates reproduced
here are, in fact, taken from
an atlas produced by the two
younger Ottens brothers,
Reiner and Josua. They took
over the family publishing
business when their father,
and founder of the firm, died
in 1725. Based in
Amsterdam they produced
atlases that were largely
compilations of maps and
charts prepared by other
cartographers. An atlas of
Dutch maps, varying from
four to fifteen volumes,
could be assembled to order.

This map of the northern
hemisphere sky includes the
Ptolemaic constellations and
a number of the newly-
designed ones. The eight
northern hemisphere
constellations, introduced by
Johannes Hevelius in the
previous century, are
depicted. Mons Maenalus (at
lower left), strictly speaking,

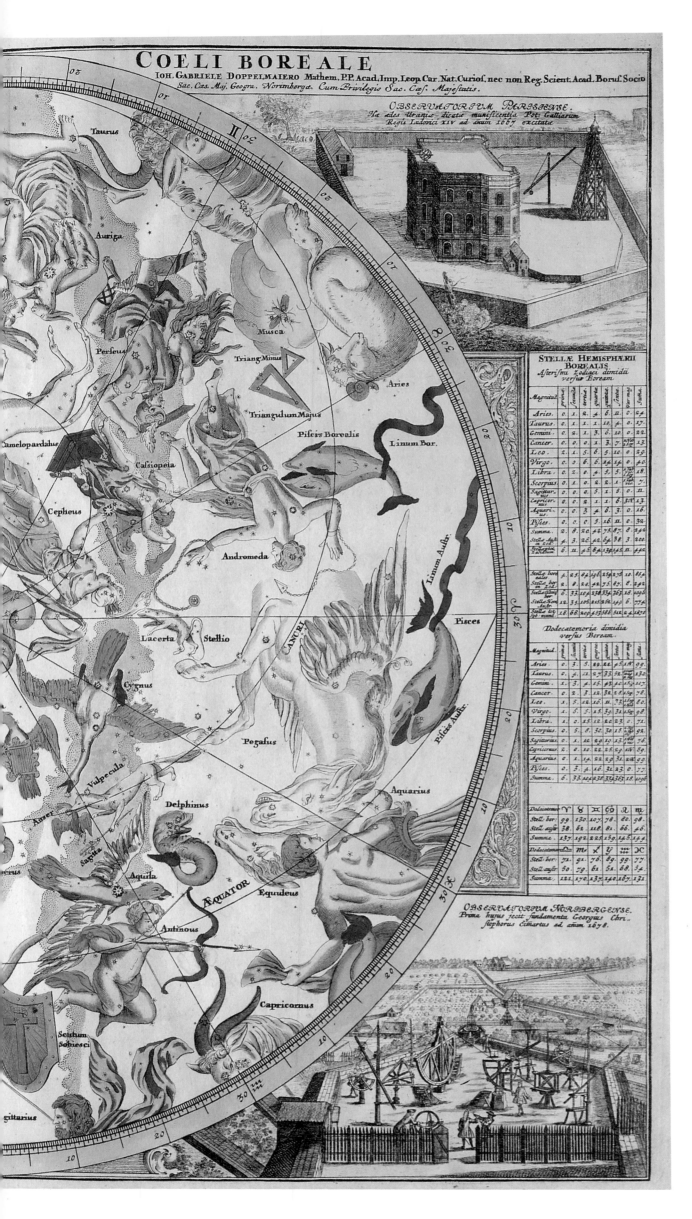

is not a constellation in its own right but a part of Boötes. Boötes is seen standing on the mountain of Arcadia in the central Peloponnese.

Around the edge of the star chart are four observatories. At top left can be seen that of Tycho Brahe on the island of Hven; at right is the observatory at Paris. Below on the left is Hevelius' observatory at Danzig; while below right can be seen that of Eimmart at Nuremberg.

The south celestial sky
from Atlas van Zeevaert en
Koophandel Door de
Geheele Weereldt *by Reiner
and Josua Ottens,
Amsterdam, 1745. Plate size
23.5 × 19.5 in.*

Star charts like this one, and
its northern sky mate, would
normally have been
produced in monotone first,
and then hand-coloured.
This meant that each
coloured map was a unique
product. The colours chosen
for one constellation could
differ from one version to
the next. The atlases and
maps produced by the
Ottens brothers were
particularly colourful.

Coloured star maps,
however, from the time of
the first printed charts by
Albrecht Dürer in 1515 to
the present day, are the
exception rather than the
rule. All the leading
astronomical atlases
depicting the constellation
figures, such as those by
Bayer, Hevelius, Flamsteed
and Bode, were produced in
black and white. Coloured
celestial atlases like those by
Cellarius and Dopplemayer,
although beautiful to look at,
were not particularly useful
to the astronomer for they
were not supported by the
necessary catalogues or
tables. Consequently the
plates used in this Ottens
atlas, were not very reliable.

This sky map shows the
southern constellations in
use in the mid-eighteenth
century. With one exception,
all the constellations
depicted here are still in use,
although they may have
been modified. Sextans
Uraniae, at lower left,
introduced by Johannes
Hevelius in memory of the
instrument with which he

made his astronomical observations, is now known simply as Sextans. Robur Carolinum, Charles's oak, introduced by Edmond Halley in 1678, was still popular in the eighteenth century; though in fact it survived into the nineteenth century, it is not now one of the 88 constellations internationally recognised today. The four observatories depicted round the edge of the star chart are those of Greenwich at top left, Copenhagen, top right, Cassel at lower left, and Berlin at lower right.

North celestial planisphere

attributed to James Barlow, London, c.1790. British Museum Collection. Plate size 14 × 14 in.

Two colourful celestial maps were produced by the British engraver, James Barlow, towards the end of the eighteenth century. While attractive they had limited scientific use, for, throughout the course of the previous two centuries, the skies of both the northern and the southern hemispheres had been recatalogued. The list of catalogued stars was growing, and their positions were being determined with greater and greater accuracy. Newly observed stars were being grouped into constellations, and some of these were now being readily accepted by the scientific and cartographic communities. No such advance is reflected in Barlow's work. It can perhaps be argued that it was his intention to produce maps that were aesthetic rather than useful in which case the old constellations would do as well as the new.

On this Northern hemisphere map, the only non-Ptolemaic constellations are Antinous, Coma Berenices, and Cor Coroli. The first two were in fact known to Ptolemy and were mentioned in his *Almagest*. Antinous was included as a sub-division of Aquila, and Coma Berenices was described as a 'nebulous mass'. However, it was not until the Dutch geographer and cartographer, Gerard Mercator, included these on his globe of 1551 that they became constellations in

their own right. Coma Berenices is still in the heavens today, Antinous fell out of use once Johann Bode incorporated its stars into the constellation of Aquila. Cor Coroli is best described as a constellation within a constellation. One of the two hunting dogs held by Boötes is drawn around a bright star known as Cor Coroli or Charles's heart, after King Charles I of England. This one-star constellation was invented by Sir Charles Scarborough, physician to King Charles II. It first appeared on a star map produced by the British cartographer, Francis Lamb in 1673.

Cetus and adjacent constellations
from Urania's Mirror.
Published by Samuel Leigh,
London, c.1825. National
Maritime Museum, London.
Plate size 8.0 × 5.5 in.

A comprehensive telescopic survey of the southern sky was made in the years 1751–1752 by the French astronomer Abbe Nicolas Louis de Lacaille. He worked from Table Mountain, at the Cape of Good Hope in southern Africa, to produce a catalogue of 9,800 stars. This was nine and a half thousand more stars than those already catalogued by Edmond Halley. When Lacaille delivered his expedition report to the Académie Royale des Sciences on 15 November 1754, he presented a large painted map. His southern hemisphere map contained 1,930 stars painted in gold on a grey background. The original map now hangs in the observatory in Paris.

Included in the map were fourteen completely new constellations devised by Lacaille himself. They featured instruments from the arts and sciences as their themes. Lacaille's work was very readily and quickly accepted, and reproduced by subsequent cartographers. Two of his constellations – Sculptor and Fornax – are shown here. All fourteen of his constellations are still in use today. They are listed here as first described by Lacaille (followed in brackets

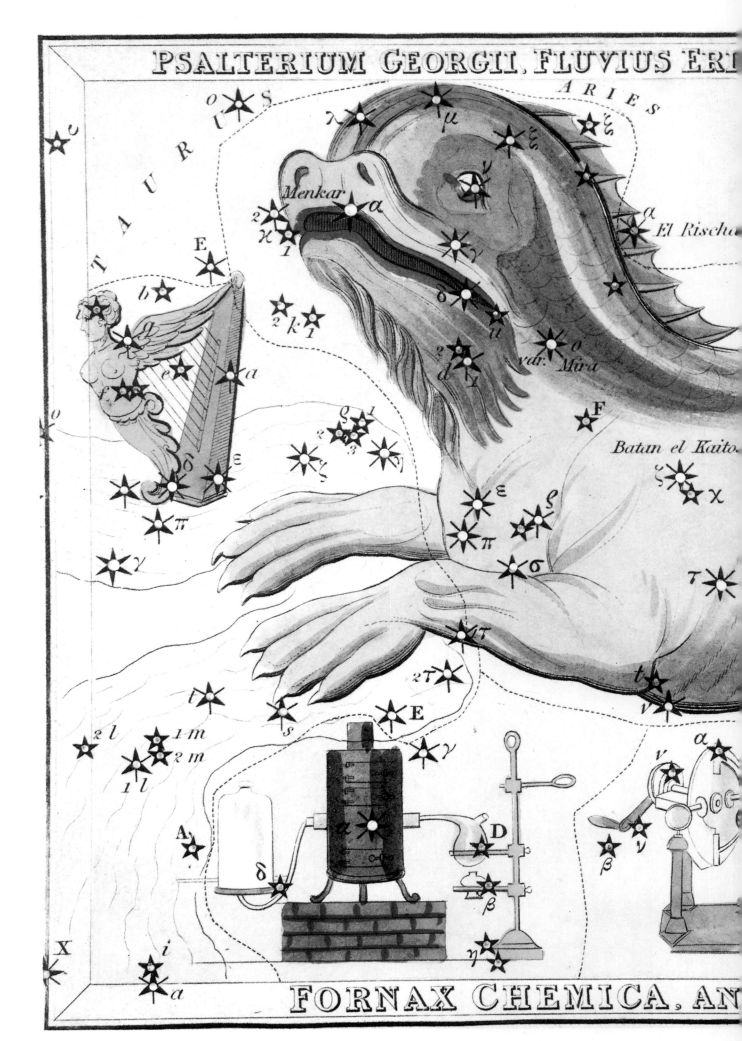

DANUS, CETUS, OFFICINA SCULPTORIS,

Pl.28.

MACHINA ELECTRICA.

by their present name and English meaning): La Machine Pneumatique (Antlia – the air pump), La Boussole (Pyxis – the mariner's compass), Le Chevalet et la Palette (Pictor – the painter's easel), Le Reticule Romboide (Reticulum – the net), L'Horloge (Horologium – the clock), Les Burins (Caelum – the engraving tool), Le Fourneau (Fornax – the furnace), L'Atelier du Sculpteur (Sculptor – the sculptor), Le Microscope (Microscopium – the microscope), Le Telescope (Telescopium – the telescope), L'Equerre et La Regle (Norma – the level), Le Compas (Circinus – the compasses), L'Octans Reflexion (Octans – the octant), and Montagne de la Table (Mensa – the table mountain).

99

South celestial planisphere

attributed to James Barlow, London, c.1790. British Museum Collection. Plate size 14 × 14 in.

Like its northern counterpart, this southern sky map by Barlow does not depict many of the constellations introduced in the hundred years before its production. None of the constellations presented by Lacaille after his thorough survey of the southern sky are included here. The most recently invented constellation appearing on this map is Robur Carolinum, the oak tree of King Charles II of England, introduced by the British astronomer, Edmond Halley, in 1678.

The other non-Ptolemaic constellations are those proposed by Petrus Plancius almost three hundred years earlier. His Columba Noachi is still in use today, but is known simply as Columba, the dove. The stars that make up this group had been known to Ptolemy. He listed them as surrounding the nearby constellation, Canis Major; but, it was not until 1592 when Plancius drew a dove around these stars that they became a constellation in their own right. The dove is generally accepted as Noah's dove; in this map it is described as such, but it could also be the dove featured in the story of the Argonauts.

Next to Columba is Argo, the galley in which Jason and the Argonauts journeyed in search of the golden fleece. The name of the constellation comes from Argus, the ship's architect and builder. When the

Argonauts were sailing through rocks guarding the Black Sea, they released a dove from the galley to help them on their route. Argo was one of the constellations known to Greek astronomers and hence listed by Ptolemy. It was renamed Noah's ark by Plancius although that change was not adopted by Barlow. Today we know it as three independent constellations; Carina, the keel, Puppis, the stern, and Vela, the sails.

The Constellations Camelopardalis, Tarandus and Custos Messium

from: Urania's Mirror. *Published by Samuel Leigh, London, c.1825. National Maritime Museum, London. Plate size 8 × 5.5 in.*

The French astronomer, Pierre Charles Le Monnier, introduced two constellations into the sky, neither of which are used today. In 1776 he devised the unusual bird, solitaire, by grouping together a number of stars lying close to the zodiacal constellation of Libra. In his original design for the constellation, engraved by Yves Marie Le Gouaz, the solitaire is depicted as a female blue rock thrush. This bird was then commonly known as the solitaire of the Philippines.

Le Monnier proposed the constellation to commemorate an expedition to the Island of Rodrigues, in the Indian Ocean, by his friend, the astronomer Abbé Alexandre-Gui Pingré. Pingré's purpose was to observe the 1761 transit of Venus across the Sun's disc, although the weather prevented him from doing so. The Island of Rodrigues was home to another solitaire, a longer legged, stouter bird than that of the Philippines. Pingré looked in vain for the bird which some years later was shown to be extinct. Why Le Monnier chose to use the Philippines' solitaire for his constellation we do not know. The same

group of stars was to appear
as a mocking bird and then a
night owl on subsequent star
maps. But not one of these
birds was adopted by either
the cartographic or the
astronomical communities.

The second of Le
Monnier's constellations also
celebrates a scientific
expedition. In the 1730s Le
Monnier had journeyed to
Lapland to measure the
length of a degree of
terrestrial latitude. On his
return he produced the
constellation Le Renne, the
reindeer, sometimes known
as Tarandus. To form this
constellation he grouped
together some northern
stars near the constellation
of Cassiopeia. Although Le
Renne does appear on some
later maps, it was not
universally adopted and no
longer features in our
northern sky.

The comet of 1742

from Atlas Novus Sive
Tabulae Geographicae,
Augsburg, c.1745. Plate size
24 × 18.5 in.

Comets are snowballs of ice
and dust which travel in
orbits from the very edge of
our solar system around the
Sun. Comets are quite small
– Halley's Comet, for
example, is about ten miles
long and five miles wide.
Close to the Sun, however,
they develop tails of gas and
dust which reflect sunlight;
these tails, which can be
hundreds of thousands of
miles in length, are visible
from Earth.

The paths of comets are
plotted against the
background of stars. This
map, which shows the path
of the comet of 1742, is
particularly beautiful. It was
produced by the German
cartographer and
instrument-maker Matthew
Seutter, who in 1727 became
Imperial Geographer.

The left-hand map shows
the comet of 1742 cutting
across the northern sky,
through the constellations of
Draco and Cepheus. This
comet was first seen from
the Cape of Good Hope
when it was south of the
celestial equator. A few days
later, on 8 February 1742, it
reached its closest to the Sun
and then started its long
journey out of the planetary
system. As February
progressed, the comet
moved into the northern
sky, and on 1 March it was
observed by Cassini in Paris.
It was then of first
magnitude, low near the
horizon with a four-degree
tail. It was observed from
Bologna throughout the
period 13 March to 15 April,
and it is this part of its path

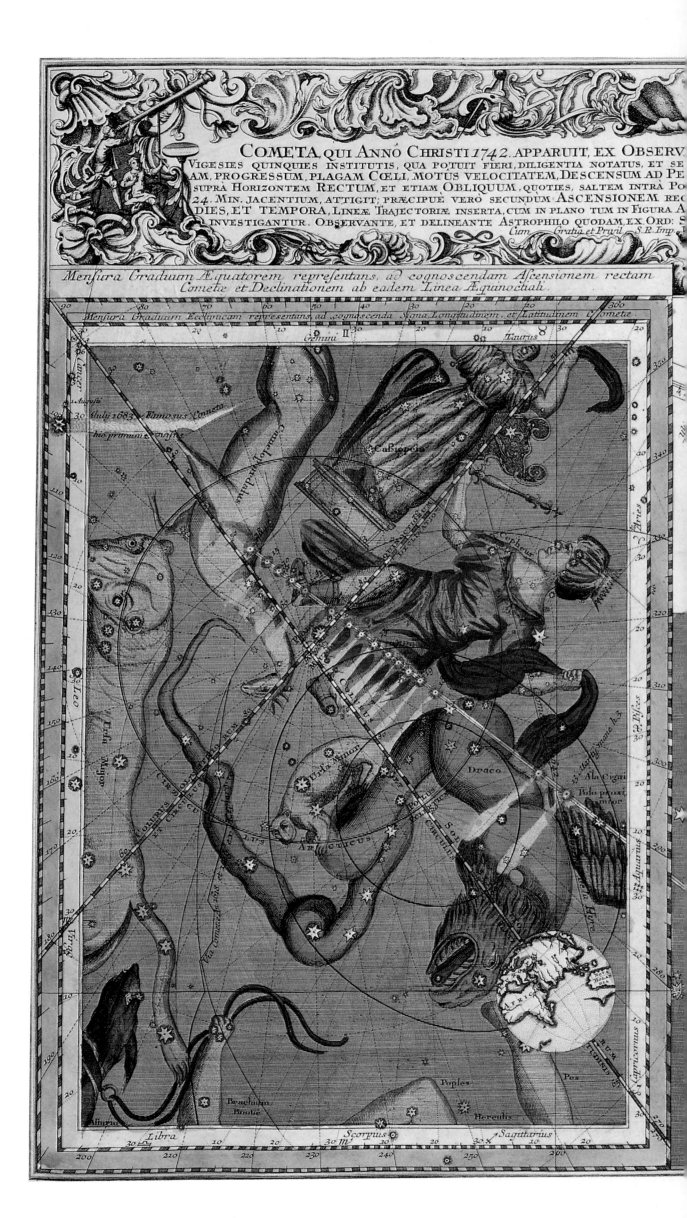

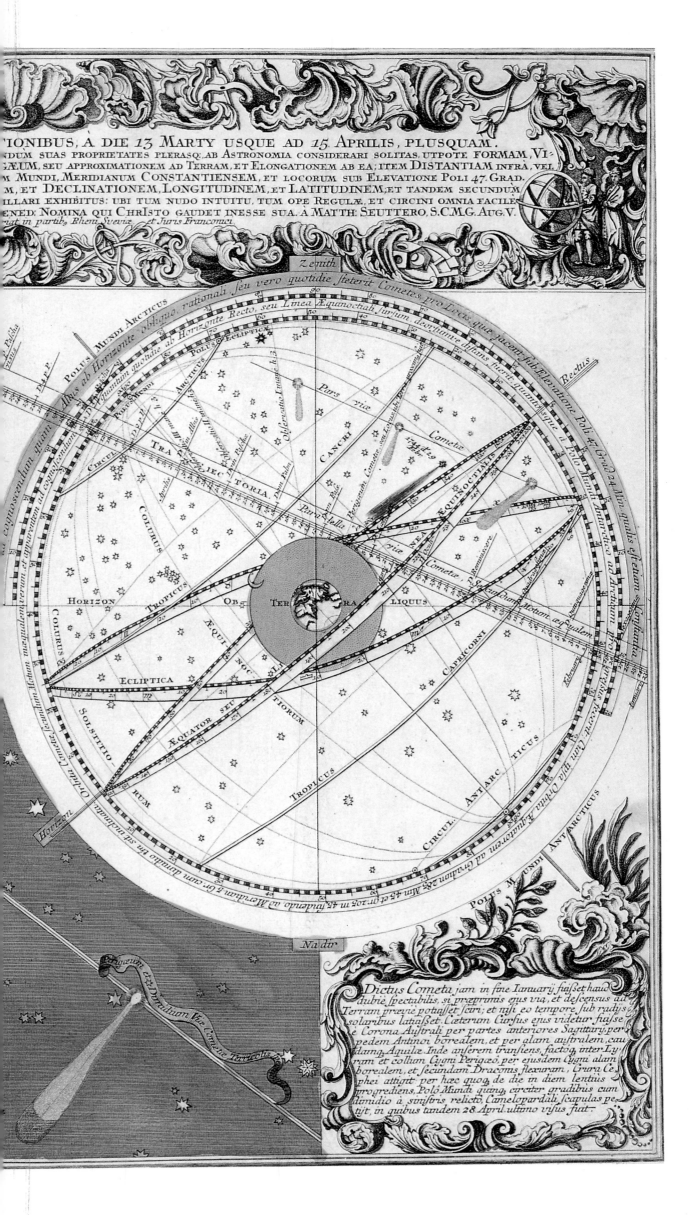

that is clearly depicted on the maps.

The right-hand figure not only presents an extended version of the path of the comet of 1742 but also shows a single position of the famous comet of 1744. This very bright comet became brighter than the planet Venus. In late February 1744, when it was only twelve degrees from the Sun, it was observed from Bologna, using a meridian circle. Daylight comets such as this are most unusual.

Three other comet tracks can be seen on these two maps – these refer to the comets of 1618 to 1619, 1642 and 1683.

The celestial sky
Anonymous, late eighteenth century. Rice-paper with material border, rollers on two edges. National Maritime Museum, London. Plate size 24.5 × 13.25 in.

Chinese astronomers developed their own system of constellations. Many of their star groupings were made from small numbers of stars, in relatively small areas of sky, and by incorporating stars left unformed in alternative constellation schemes. Consequently there are many more Chinese than Western constellations – as early as the third century AD, 283 constellations had been formed from a total of 1,464 stars. Many of the designs, which depicted Chinese life, were intricate, and only a very good observer working on a clear night would have had a chance of matching the constellations to the night sky above.

Stars in the constellation of Cepheus were depicted as a charioteer and chariot; the army of Yu Lin was formed from stars in south-eastern Aquarius; and a Chinese serpent was in the northernmost part of Cygnus. The Chinese emperor, his secretaries and the court eunuchs were also in the sky. In addition to the long list of smaller constellations, there were four much larger constellations which incorporated many of the smaller ones. These four superconstellations

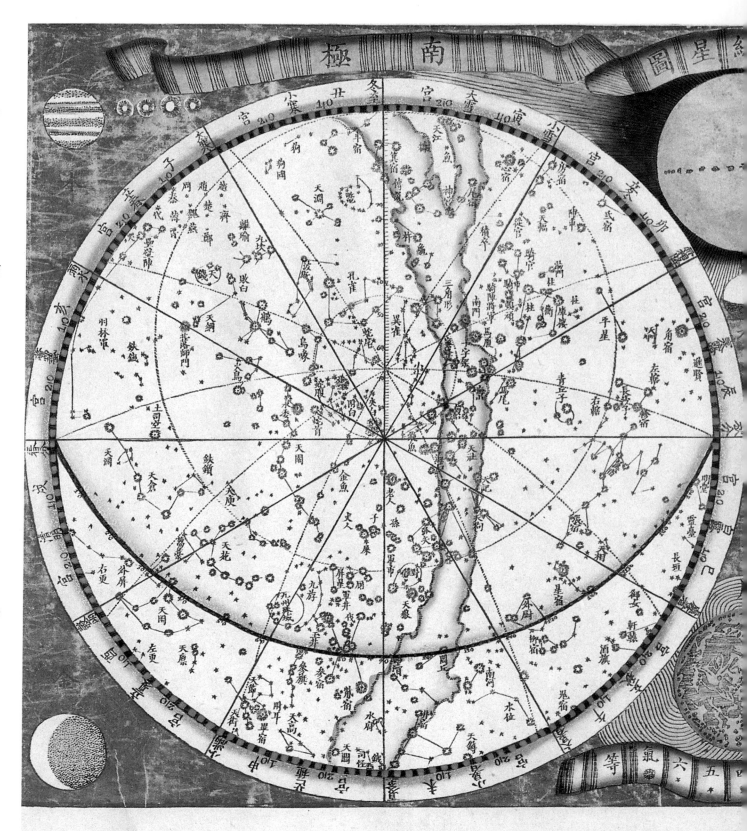

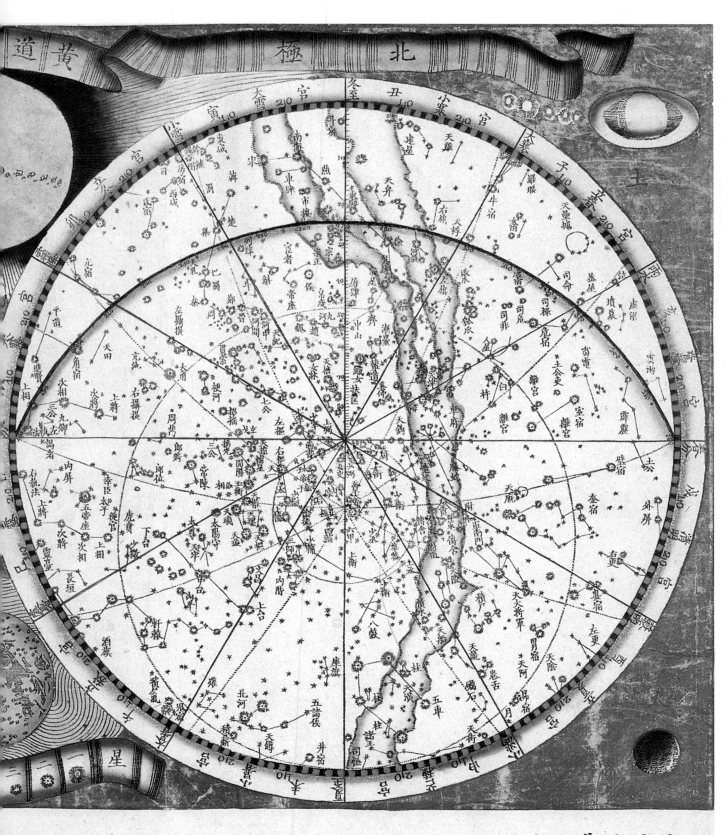

symbolised the seasons.
Spring was represented by
the blue dragon, Ts'ang-
Loung; summer was the red
bird, Tchou-Niao; autumn
was the white tiger; and
winter was the black
tortoise, Hiouen-Woo.

The northern celestial sky
appears on the right of this
map; the southern on the
left. The path of the Milky
Way stands out on both
planispheres. Planets
surround the star maps. The
most distant planets then
known – Jupiter (upper left)
and Saturn (upper right) –
are shown with their
satellite systems. The three
outer planets had not yet
been discovered: Uranus was
discovered in 1781, Neptune
in 1846 and Pluto in 1930.

七政體象太陽之面有小
莫可紀極兩星圖外又有
天漢之內聚集無數小星
微此類星形大約隱見於
理即習知天文者亦難明
見有隱見又不一假如舊而今反
今偏隱又是舊隱而今稍
有隱見又不一假如舊而
又週天星形自古迄今稍
星每日旋行一週天之數
極查看赤道經度得識恒
虛線相交至赤道南北兩
至三百六十度每三十度
一在北圖從初度至一百八十度
圖從初度至一百八十度
圖上有赤道分界一在南
約積七十一年瀟行一度大
西往東定行五十一秒大
從無變更其經度每年自
為恒星緯度但恒星之緯
度按度查恒星經度以丑
宮線至中心又分為九十度
節氣隨之每宮分為三十
線分為十二宮邊列宮名
為兩極外圈為黃道以直
黃道南北兩總星圖中心

The constellations Monoceros, Canis Minor and Atelier Typographique
from Urania's Mirror. *Published by Samuel Leigh, London, c. 1825. National Maritime Museum, London. Plate size 8 × 5.5 in.*

During the course of the nineteenth century, celestial atlases moved away from a decorative to a more functional style. Astronomers and map-makers were concentrating more closely on the straightforward astronomical information to be included in a map: on a star's magnitude and its precise location, rather than on its pictorial representation which, although very attractive, could interfere with the needs of the map's user.

Decisions had to be made about how many astronomical objects could be included in one atlas. As more celestial objects were catalogued, and new ones were discovered, the maps were in danger of becoming more and more cluttered. For astronomers the constellation drawings were not essential and could be excluded, but they remained popular with members of the public who were not so familiar with the night sky. For them, simpler star maps were produced, incorporating the most easily viewed naked-eye stars and including the constellation patterns.

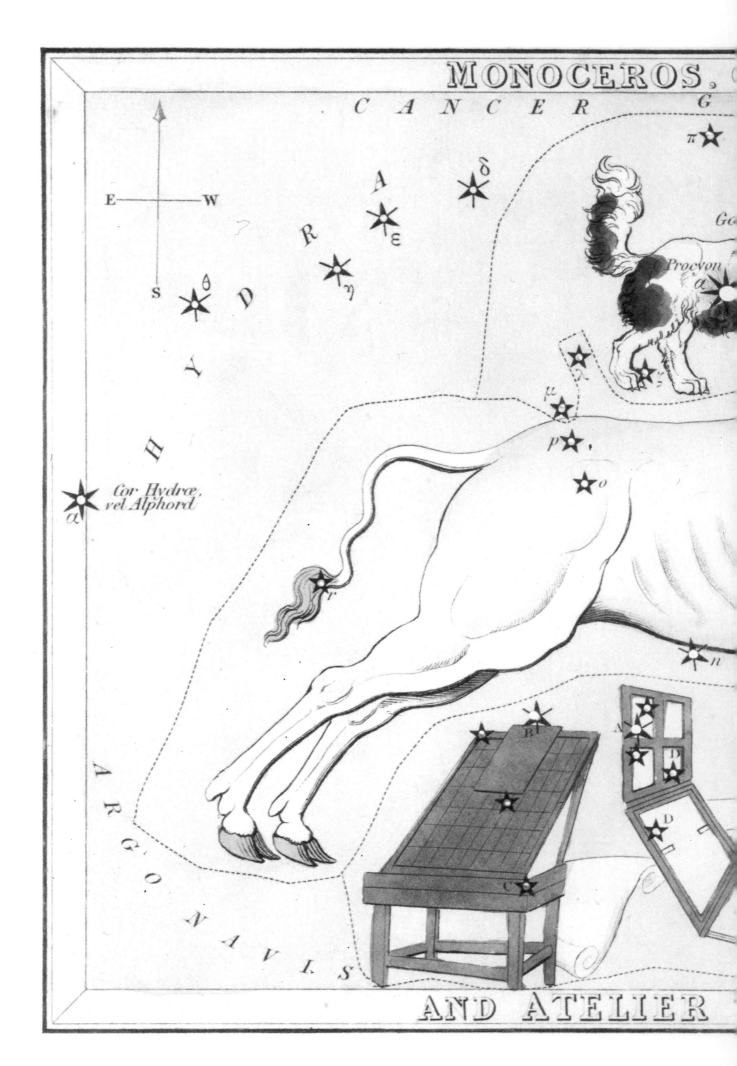

Johann Elert Bode's *Uranographia*, published at the very start of the century, in 1801, was one of the last great decorative constellation atlases. It included eighteen maps concentrating on the major constellations, and two hemispheres. Together they incorporated 17,240 individual stars with magnitudes ranging from one to eight, as well as double stars, nebulae and star clusters.

The observations had been made by almost thirty astronomers. A substantial number of northern star positions – 12,000 in all – were provided by the French astronomer Lalande, who had been observing from Paris. Bode also used the work of another French astronomer, Lacaille, who had systematically surveyed the southern sky. The constellation figures that Bode used had been devised by various cartographers and astronomers, but he also introduced a number of his own. This illustration includes Atelier Typographique, which Bode described as 'Officina Typographica'. He introduced it in his 1801 atlas to commemorate the 350th anniversary of Gutenberg's invention of movable type.

Hydra and adjacent constellations
from Urania's Mirror. *Published by Samuel Leigh, London, c.1825. National Maritime Museum, London. Size 8 × 5.5 in.*

A novel way of presenting both the stars and their constellation patterns was devised in the 1820s for a set of 32 hand-coloured cards published by Samuel Leigh and known collectively as *Urania's Mirror*. The stars are marked by tiny holes in the cards, which have a tissue-paper backing. When the cards are lit from behind, they appear like bright lights in a dark sky – just as in real life. Light the cards from the front and the observer can see the constellation patterns printed on them, which will help him to become familiar with the night sky.

Each card depicts either a major constellation or several closely related ones. The constellation boundaries, the relative brightness of the stars and the names of the major stars are all given. Some of the constellations depicted were short-lived. Globus aerostaticus – the hot-air balloon, proposed by the French astronomer Joseph Jerome de Lalande in salute to the pioneering balloonists the Montgolfier brothers – is no longer in the sky, nor is Felis, his cat, shown here at centre right. Both of these constellations were first presented in Johann Bode's atlas of 1801.

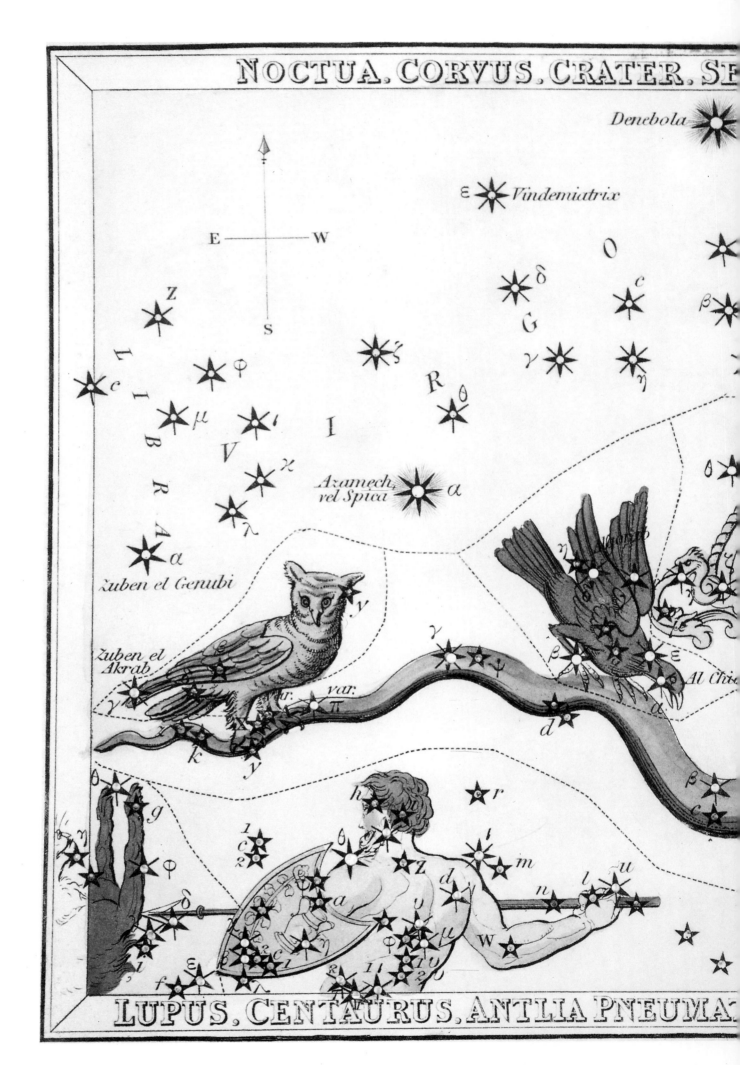

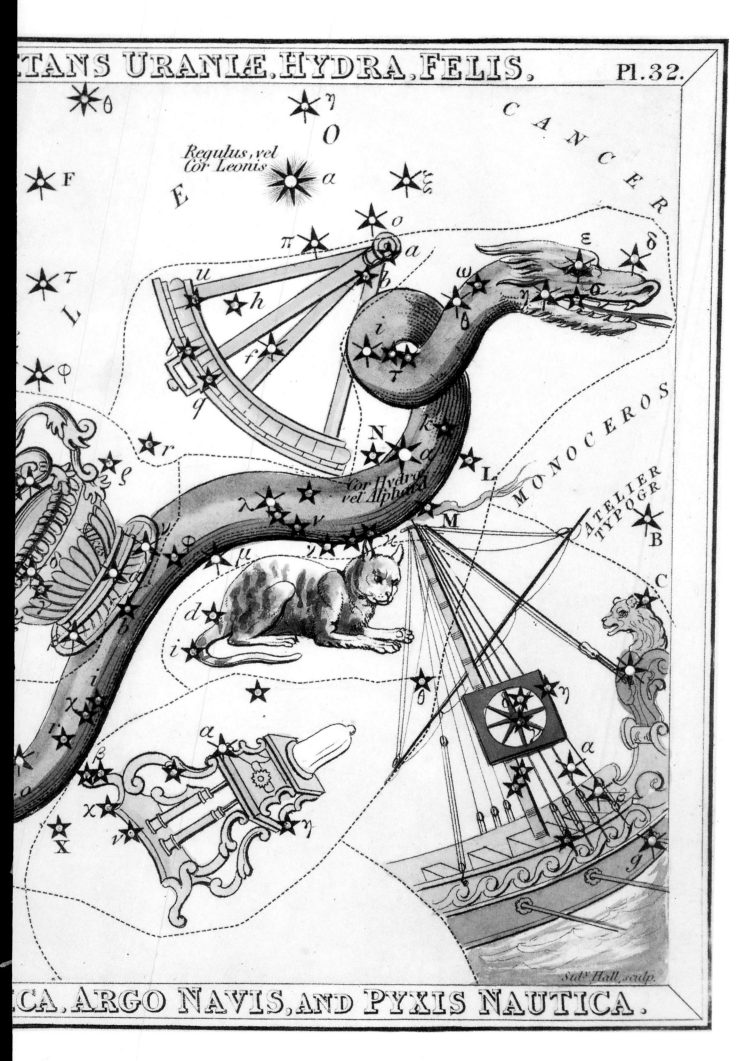

CA, ARGO NAVIS, AND PYXIS NAUTICA.

The name of the engraver, Sidney Hall, appears on each card, though another hand is thought to have been responsible for the explanatory booklet written to accompany the cards but which has often been separated from them in the intervening years. The author is said to have been Jehoshaphat Aspin. Mystery also surrounds the originator of the cards, who, according to the booklet, was 'A Lady'. Whoever was responsible, the cards offer an attractive and easy way of becoming familiar with the heavens.

Celestial planisphere for use in the northern hemisphere

by Jehoshaphat Aspin, London, c.1840. National Maritime Museum, London. Diameter 14.6 in.

This planisphere was devised by Jehoshaphat Aspin and published on his behalf by James Wyld ('Geographer to the Queen and Prince Albert'), and Grant & Griffith in London. Practically the only thing we know about Aspin is that he was interested in popularising the heavens. This planisphere would help identify the date and time at which the constellations in the northern sky would be visible. His thirty-two card set, *Urania's Mirror*, would present these constellations in even greater detail. Both observing aids were accompanied by handbooks. Aspin's 112-page *Familiar Treatise on Astronomy*,

produced for use with the cards, gave information on all the constellations he depicted, as well as covering the solar system. The booklet accompanying this planisphere described how best it could be used.

Aspin's work includes some interesting constellations. At centre left appears Telescopium Herschelii which celebrates the discovery of the planet Uranus by William Herschel in 1781. As a direct result of the discovery of Uranus, Herschel received patronage from King George III of England, also commemorated on this planisphere. At lower left is Psalterium Georgii, George's harp. Both constellations were originally introduced by the Austrian astronomer Maximilian Hell in 1789. Neither of these constellations appear in the sky today.

The northern sky

from Atlas Coelestis seu Harmonica Macrocosmica *by Andreas Cellarius, Amsterdam, 1661. Plate size 20.75 × 17.5 in.*

Identifying a star within a constellation can be a problem. Astronomers need to be sure that they are referring to the same star when they compare their observations. Quoting a star's coordinates would certainly help to avoid any confusion. But other, quicker, methods of identification, relating to the brighter stars within a constellation, have developed. Bayer's letters and Flamsteed's numbers are used to identify stars. But the brightest can also be known by their individual names. Some, like Polaris and Sirius, are popularly better known by their names than by their Greek letter and parent constellation – α Ursae Minoris and α Canis Majoris, respectively.

There is a long tradition of naming stars. Sirius, and Arcturus (α Boötes, see map) were both used by Ptolemy and are of Greek origin. Sirius, which is the brightest star in the whole sky, stems from the ancient Greek for 'scorching one' or 'brilliant one'. Arcturus comes from 'bear watcher' describing its proximity to the great bear. Ptolemy also referred to stars by their position within a constellation, Leo was described as 'the star on the end of the tail'. Ptolemy's work was translated into Arabic a number of times in the eighth and ninth centuries, and in translation this description became 'dhanab-al-asad'. This was westernised into Denebola,

RIUM STEL REALE QVUM.

the star's present name.

Other star names have a more truly Arabic origin, Almach (γ Andromeda, see map) and Aldebaran (α Tauri, see map) fall into this category. Almach started off as 'anaq al-ard', meaning, in the Middle East, a black-eared cat. This became 'alamac' in medieval Latin. Later scholars assumed the source was the Arabic word for boot, 'al-muq', and thus Almach was born. Aldebaran is more straightforward, its source is Arabic for 'follower', possibly referring to its position in the sky behind the Pleiades (see map).

The southern sky
from Atlas Coelestis seu
Harmonica Macrocosmica *by*
Andreas Cellarius,
Amsterdam, 1661. Plate size
20.75 × 17.5 in.

Around two hundred and
fifty individual stars have
names today, although only
a fraction of these are in
common use. The majority
of these names originated
with the Arabs or the Greeks
who in turn inherited some
from the Babylonians or
Sumerians. Over the
centuries all these names
have evolved together and
their origin is not always
entirely clear.

Some of the star names
that we now use may sound
Arabic though they may
have little or no origin in
Arabic works. Betelgeuse,
the current name for
α Orionis has had a number
of variants. All of them were
bad guess-translations of the
Arabic 'yad al-jawza', 'the
hand of al Jawza', or 'Orion',
which itself had been a poor
translation of Ptolemy's
description, 'the shoulder of
Orion', which describes the
star accurately.

Identified on the previous
map is Spica (α Virginis)
which comes from the
Roman for 'the ear of grain'.
This can be traced back to
the Babylonians and
Sumerians. Fomalhaut,
α Piscis Austrinis, is named
on this map. It is not unusual
to find these two names on
star maps; they are two of
the twenty brightest stars in
the entire sky. However, the
inclusion of other star names
is less obvious. The choice is
often left with the
cartographer, and, on the
less scientific maps, this can
seem totally arbitrary.

Constellations contain

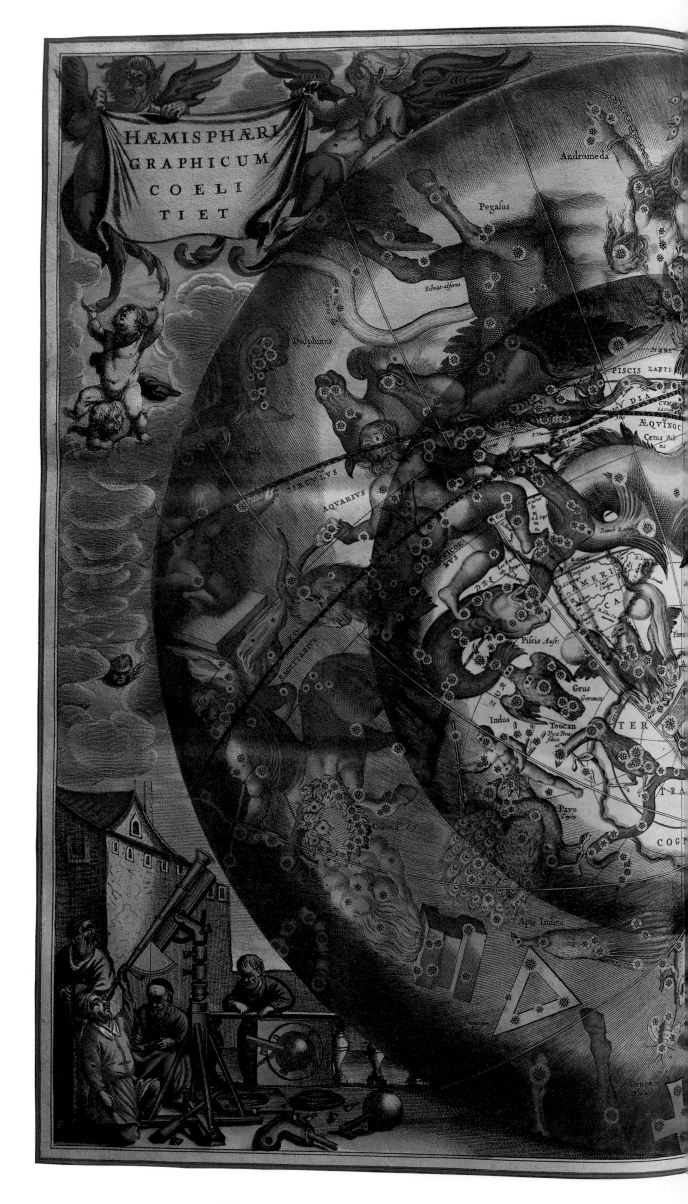

more than single stars. As new classifications were discovered, methods of identifying them on maps were developed. Star clusters, nebulous gas clouds and galaxies are now known by their 'M' or 'NGC' number. Neither of these systems refers to the parent constellation. The 'M' numbers were assigned by the French astronomer, Charles *Messier*, in the late eighteenth century. The 'NGC' numbers come from the *New General Catalogue*, first published in 1888, and listing thousands of objects. A star cluster, such as the Pleiades, would today probably be marked on a map as M45; on maps printed before and for some years after Messier's listing, its name would probably be written out in full.

The term 'planisphere' is popularly used for two distinct but closely related types of star map. Today the term is understood to mean a circular star map printed on card or plastic and covered by a similar piece of material. The covering disc has a window which, as the disc revolves, reveals sections of the star map. The two discs can be positioned for a chosen time and date. The stars then appearing in the window are those visible in the sky at that time. The star map of this type of planisphere, centred on either the north or the south celestial pole, covers the sky visible from a particular latitude during the course of a year. Planispheres are produced for a number of latitudes and are readily available. Wherever you live, you should be able to find an inexpensive and easy-to-use star map which will help you enjoy the night sky.

The term 'planisphere' is also used, as it has been in this book, to describe circular star maps depicting the stars of either the northern or southern hemisphere. Together they show the whole of the celestial sky.

The card planisphere shown here was produced for the north American market which centred on Philadelphia. It includes three interesting constellations of 'honour', none of which are in use today. In 1688 the German

astronomer, Godfried Kirch, introduced the Brandenburg sceptre, Sceptrum Brandenburgicum, to honour the province of that name. Honores Frederici was proposed by Johann Bode in 1787 to honour King Frederick the Great of Prussia. Harpa Georgii, close to Taurus, was introduced in 1789 as Psalterium Georgianum by the astronomer Maximilian Hell. Johann Bode changed it to Harpa Georgii in his 1801 atlas. It is in honour of King George III of England.

Planisphere with the path of Donati's Comet
published by Waller and Deacon, London, October 5th, 1858. National Maritime Museum, London. Plate size 12 × 13 in.

Maps of the sky, particularly those in the form of an adjustable planisphere, so popular in the later nineteenth and twentieth centuries, acted as backdrops for other celestial objects. This planisphere was produced specifically for the 1858 sighting of Donati's Comet. It was not intended for use by the professional astronomical community, but by the amateur astronomer. The apparently sudden appearance of a celestial visitor in the night sky produced an upsurge of interest in astronomy in 1858, much as it did when Halley's Comet returned in 1910 and again in 1985 to 1986. Simple planispheres plotting the comet's course against the sky would provide the basic information necessary for the novice observer.

The Italian astronomer, Giovanni Battista Donati, discovered the great comet that is named after him on June 2nd 1858. At that time, the comet was seen as a feeble round nebulous cloud in the constellation of Leo. It became visible to the naked eye at the end of August, and during September it began to develop into one of the most impressive comets of the century. By September 6th, it had a distinctive curved tail and by 16th the comet's head outshone the brightest stars in Ursa Major. The comet came closest to the Earth on October 10th; the tail was seen to stretch 60°

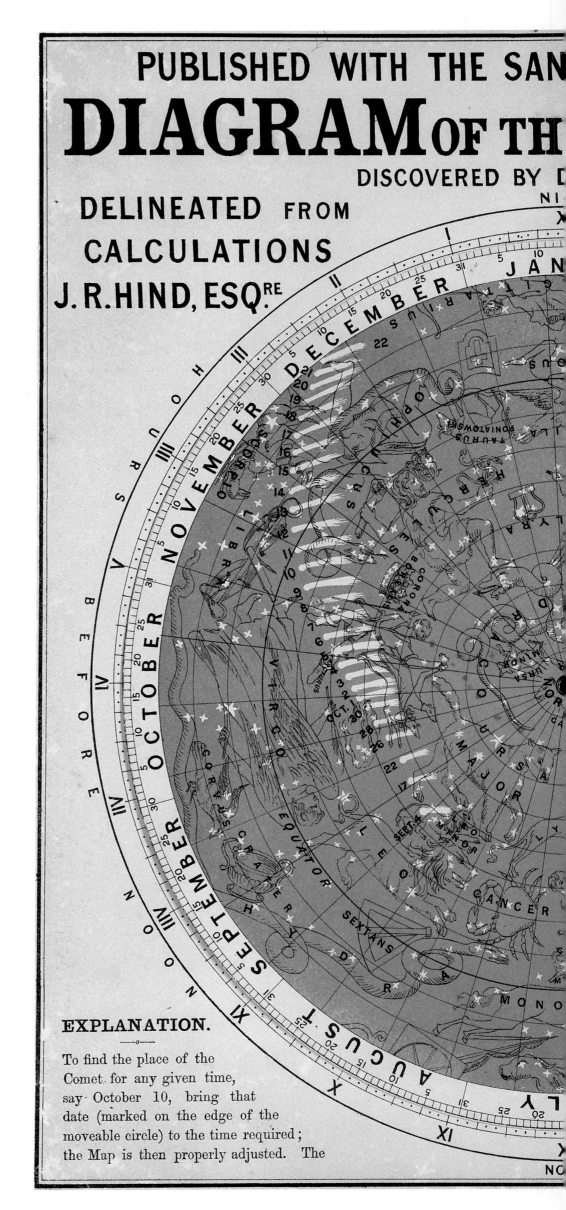

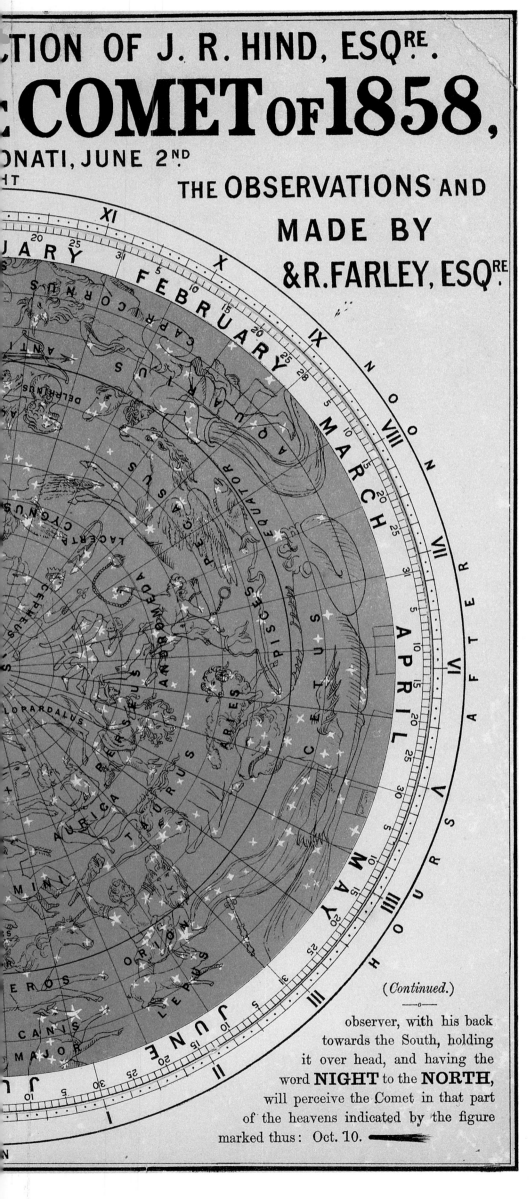

CTION OF J. R. HIND, ESQ^{RE}.

COMET OF 1858,

NATI, JUNE 2ND

THE OBSERVATIONS AND
MADE BY
&R.FARLEY, ESQ^{RE}.

(Continued.)

observer, with his back
towards the South, holding
it over head, and having the
word **NIGHT** to the **NORTH**,
will perceive the Comet in that part
of the heavens indicated by the figure
marked thus: Oct. 10.

across the sky in a
magnificent scimitar-like
curve. In addition to the
brilliant curved tail, two
fainter, luminous trains were
observed. After that, the
comet proceeded to fade
quickly, disappearing from
naked-eye view around
November 8th.

John Russell Hind was an
English astronomer who had
himself discovered a comet
in 1847, and written a book
on comets, which was
published in 1852.

The celestial sky
entitled Sarvasiddhantatatt-vacudamani *or* Jewel of the Essence of All Sciences *by Durgasankara Pathaka, India, 1840. British Library, Oriental Manuscript 5289 (folios 56 and 57). Plate size 20 × 16 in.*

With very few exceptions, the celestial maps and illustrations reproduced in this book elucidate the story behind the system of constellations designed and accepted by western astronomers and cartographers, and adopted by today's international scientific community. Independent systems were also developed, whereby the celestial sky was divided into areas, and the grouped stars formed the basis of an easily recognised picture. But these systems were never adopted outside their country of origin, and are not used by professional astronomers today.

The ancient Indian astronomers did not produce star catalogues as did the ancient Greeks and Chinese. Yet they were interested, for their work on calendars, in those stars that formed a backdrop to the motions of the Sun and Moon. These Indian astronomers divided the ecliptic into twenty-eight naksatras, each one about 13° in length. Away from the

zodiac band, they recognised a few star groupings, and named some of the brighter stars.

The zodiac band of constellations dominate these two Indian planispheres, but they show the western European system of constellations even though each is drawn in Indian costume and style. On the right, running from bottom to top are Sagittarius, Capricornus, Aquarius, Pisces, Aries and Taurus. On the left, running from top to bottom are Gemini, Cancer, Leo, Virgo, Libra and Scorpio. They are surrounded by other western constellations. The use of the western system reflects perhaps the presence of the British in India from the early nineteenth century.

The manuscript was produced as part of an astrological horoscope. Certainly it offers no astronomical information, but no one can argue that it is not a most attractive celestial chart. The horoscope was prepared by Pathaka of Benares for Prince Navanihal Singh at the behest of his father, Khadga Singh.

Celestial globe
*by Georama Ltd, London,
1989. Private collection.
Diameter 30 in.*

In the early years of the
twentieth century, the
London-based publishing
house of George Philip took
over the globe-making firm,
Smiths, which had
manufactured both
terrestrial and celestial
globes during the previous
century. The globes were
usually 12 to 15 inches in
diameter, although larger
ones were also produced.
These two illustrations show
sections of a 30-inch Smith
globe. A subsidiary of George
Philip, named Georama,
produced this globe in 1989
by making and assembling
lithographic copies of
Smith's original globe gores.
This was the first time that
the gores had been used
since 1948. The monotone
globe gores were hand-
coloured and then varnished
by the globe conservator
Paul Cook. For inspiration he
turned to the coloured
constellation figures of
earlier years.

This globe is inscribed:
'Containing all the principal
stars compiled from works
of Woollaston, Flamsted, de
La Caille, Hevelius, Mayer,
Bradley, Herschel,
Maskelyne, the Transactions
of the Astronomical Society
of London etc. Published by
George Philip of Fleet Street,
London'. Stellar cartography
has moved on since this
celestial globe was first
produced, and more recent
catalogues have replaced
those of the astronomers
listed here. The set of
constellation figures drawn
around the stars has also
changed. This globe includes
fine illustrations of

constellations that were introduced by the French astronomer Lacaille in 1754. The air-pump (Antlia), the mariner's compass (Pyxis) and the painter's easel (Pictor) are all on the illustration at left. A handsome clock (Horologium), a furnace (Fornax) and the sculptor (Sculptor) appear at right. These constellations are still in use today; but Felis the cat, at left, and the electrical machine, at right, are no longer in the heavens.

Georama has recently ceased production, and so the globe illustrated here proved to be their penultimate product in this line.

Celestial planisphere for use in the northern hemisphere,
by Henry Whitall, Philadelphia, 1856. National Maritime Museum, London. Plate size 15.5 × 15.5 in.

The basic idea behind the planisphere was developed at least two thousand years ago. This idea was incorporated into the planispheric astrolabe, from which today's planisphere is directly descended. Cardboard planispheres were developed in the nineteenth century to satisfy a growing interest in astronomy. Stargazing was a popular pastime, and a planisphere like the one shown here would help identify the constellations above. Before street lights lit up the night sky, the stars could be easily seen from any town. Today it is necessary to get out in the country to really appreciate the splendour of the heavens.

Planispheres were very popular; the one shown here is the third edition of this version, and it is the fourth edition of another Whitall planisphere reproduced on pages 118 and 119. It is interesting to see that Whitall produced planispheres in these two distinct styles. It would be much easier to identify the stars with this star map, than with the light-coloured one.

The nineteenth century saw a move away from the decorative style of star maps; increasingly the outlines of the figures were omitted and more utilitarian maps were produced. For the professional astronomer, the catalogues listing necessary

126

information on astronomical objects remained important. Fainter and fainter stars and new categories of object were included. Between 1859 and 1862, the Bonner Durchmusterung catalogue, containing 324,189 stars with accompanying charts, was produced. In the closing years of the century a photographic atlas of the entire sky was first attempted. More recent ones have taken its place. Widely used today is the Smithsonian Astrophysical Observatory Star Catalogue and its computer-plotted atlas. Satellites are now involved in plotting the positions of the stars with ever-increasing accuracy. Although the end-result is a better product for the working astronomer, today's maps certainly lack the charm and artistic appeal of their ancestors.

LIST OF PLATES

PHOTOGRAPH CREDITS